Klausbernd Vollmar spent many years training to interpret the Enneagram in the tradition of Gurdjieff, and has become one of the system's foremost exponents. He lives in the UK and holds workshops all over Europe.

The Secret of Enneagrams

MAPPING THE PERSONALITY

Klausbernd Vollmar

ELEMENT

Shaftesbury, Dorset • Rockport, Massachusetts

Brisbane, Queensland

© Element Books Limited 1997
© 1993 by Wilhelm Goldmann Verlag GmbH, München
Original German text

Published in the USA in 1997 by
Element Books, Inc.
PO Box 830, Rockport, MA 01966

First published in Great Britain in 1997 by
Element Books Limited
Shaftesbury, Dorset SP7 8BP

Published in Australia in 1997 by
Element Books Limited
for Jacaranda Wiley Limited
33 Park Road, Milton, Brisbane 4064

Translated by Matthew Barton
Cover design by Max Fairbrother
Design by Footnote Graphics
Typeset by Footnote Graphics, Warminster, Wilts.
Printed and bound in the USA by Edwards Brothers, Inc.

British Library Cataloguing in Publication
data available

Library of Congress Cataloging in Publication
data available

ISBN 1-85230-968-7

Contents

List of Illustrations

For Diane von Weltzien in gratitude

Go – not knowing where;
bring – not knowing what;
the path is long, the way unknown;
the hero knows how to arrive there by himself alone.

G I Gurdjieff

———

The Enneagram is the fundamental hieroglyph
of a universal language
which has as many possible meanings
as there are people at different stages.

P D Ouspensky

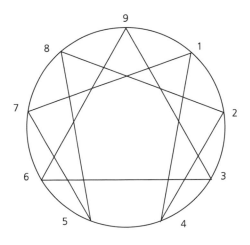

9   The reader applies it

Figure 1   *The Enneagram of this book's contents*

Foreword

At the beginning of the eighties, after living for a while in the Ruhrgebiet in Germany, in Montreal and in New York, I moved to the end of the world – to north Norfolk. In this rural region time seems to have come to a stop: nothing much has changed since the end of the 19th century. It was in this quiet place that I found a teacher who taught me much of what can be found in the pages of this book. He himself had been a pupil of Madame Jeanne de Salzmann, who ran a famous Gurdjieff group in Paris; so he had had first-hand experience of the work of George Ivanovich Gurdjieff.

At another 'end of the world', in Findhorn on the coast of northern Scotland, I had started my Enneagram studies at the beginning of the seventies, using all sorts of coloured diagrams and drawings; but I had to wait 15 years before the practical applications of this work became real experience for me – quite unexpectedly, and in a tiny, romantic village. Before I get to grips with the Enneagram itself, I would like to share a few personal thoughts about the work of Gurdjieff, to give my readers some idea about it.

In contrast to all other fashionable spiritual movements and doctrines that I know of, the Gurdjieff work starts by making the pupil realize her* failings and shortcomings. She is shown what sort of illusions she harbours about her present stage of development. No matter how positive or open I felt when I

*rather than using both masculine and feminine forms throughout, I will alternate from chapter to chapter.

attended my group, my teacher always made me feel that I was incompetent, living in a fantasy world. This sort of approach contrasts radically with the often rather naïve 'positive thinking' championed nowadays. In my Gurdjieff group I frequently felt cut down to size; but finally I realized that the aim of this – just as in depth-psychology – was to help me gain insight into my condition. The real work can only begin when I see that I am continually deceiving myself.

I am especially deluding myself – unconsciously – when I believe I can complete a task in a disciplined way, that I am able to carry out my own aims. But if I realize that I am actually capable of nothing, then the motivation to work on myself develops by itself. We need this motivation to achieve a truly positive approach and attitude.

Nowadays I consider it a healthy sign that Gurdjieff groups don't jump on fashionable spiritual bandwagons; I know now that, as C G Jung said, all spiritual work begins with the shadow-side of human nature. Such 'shadow' work offers a reliable path towards the light. I am particularly grateful to my teacher for this insight, for his help in freeing me from illusions. I have always sought a path of wisdom that would be right for my central-European consciousness; and this is what I finally found in the Gurdjieff work.

This book encapsulates my personal understanding of such work, and my personal experience with the Enneagram. Rather than dogmatically reproducing the ideas of Gurdjieff, Ouspensky, Bennett and all the schools of the Fourth Way,[1] I have relied upon my own creative understanding. All questions, pointers, tips and observations in this book are intended as stimulus and encouragement for the process of discovery. They are not meant to teach or instruct.

After my own intensive study of the Enneagram I suddenly had the feeling that I knew – at last – what I wanted from life; at the same time I also had an inkling of how to realize my aims. In the workshops and courses which I gave on the Enneagram, it gave me great pleasure to find that others shared this experience. I hope that this book may help you progress towards inner clarity and to a new understanding of yourself and your actions.

And one more introductory remark: on page 4 of this book you will find explanations and directions for the so-called 'self-remembering' exercises. If you try to be mindful of yourself as often as possible as you read this book, you will understand the Enneagram at a deeper level. Allow yourself to be touched by what you read: it is not only the head that understands; the heart also shares in the process.

The Enneagram as mystery

The Enneagram is a cosmic symbol for a higher power whose influence can be felt as a creative, life-giving force in all realms of earthly existence. This book is an attempt to liberate it from the Christian-cum-psychological strait-jacket in which it was confined some years ago, when – perhaps unfortunately – it become widely known and popularized. We will see that Gurdjieff looked upon the Enneagram above all as a tool for helping people take decisions and make plans for the future.

Gurdjieff first introduced the Enneagram in 1916, in his Moscow and St Petersburg study group, as a universal diagram of dynamic movement sequences. Since Gurdjieff did not wholly trust language – even his own – as a medium for communicating his teachings, he made wide use of diagrams, of which the Enneagram is the most fundamental. Six years later, in 1922, in his 'Institute for the Harmonious Development of Man' in Fontainebleau, he combined the Enneagram with specific movement sequences, so making it into a choreographic form.

Although Gurdjieff's teachings gained wide circulation, the Enneagram was known only to a small circle of initiates, who kept things under their hat. Gurdjieff categorically forbade the members of his Moscow and St Petersburg group from making and publishing drawings of it.

Knowledge of the Enneagram was still kept very secret until quite recently. People knew of its existence, but the only way of gaining access to it was exclusively by word of mouth, from a teacher running a group. Such groups are so breathtakingly serious that few people have the patience and endurance to keep at it until the Enneagram teaching is at last revealed to them. In one typical situation, which I experienced many years ago in an American Gurdjieff group, we asked our teacher whether he could divulge more detailed information to us about the Enneagram. In response he frowned with the sort of sorrowful smile that was customary to him and said sharply: 'First you will need to work very hard for a couple of years, until you realize that you know nothing. If you begin to suffer deeply from your lack of knowledge, you may – perhaps – become ready and open for the Enneagram teaching. The Enneagram is, in any case, only to be understood through movement. Mr Gurdjieff saw it as a key to specific knowledge that can put a new stage of consciousness within reach. But it's a long road to get there.' He then ended the session with an unanswerable 'Any more questions?' and left the room.

'Gurdjieff's movement exercises' was a magical phrase that had a fascinating resonance for outsiders. These legendary movement sequences served ultimately to help people become conscious of their own, and thereby of the cosmic, centre of movement, and to pass on ancient esoteric knowledge. Many of these movements have their source in the Enneagram. Their precise sequences not only make visible the cosmic laws expressed in it, but simultaneously affect and harmonize the emotional, physical and thought centres of the dancer.

In Gurdjieff's ballet, *The Struggle of the Magicians*, which was never performed, the throne of the White Magician stood in the middle of the Enneagram. The dancers moved along the lines of its inner hexagon. Many movement sequences of this ballet later found their way into Gurdjieff's exercise 'movements'.

His attention was first drawn to this sort of complex physical movement when he came to Tiflis in 1883 and befriended an Armenian theologian called Sarkis Pogossian. Gurdjieff continued to develop these exercises and apply them to the Enneagram throughout his life.

In spite of all the secrecy surrounding it, a book about the Enneagram has been available since 1974, written by the mathematician and long-time student of Gurdjieff, John Godolphin Bennett (1897–1974).[2] Bennett had met Gurdjieff in 1920 and became one of the most important followers of his teaching. He studied the Enneagram for 50 years before publishing something about it. At that time no one else had written about this cosmic diagram apart from Piotr Demianovich Ouspensky (1877–1947) who mentioned it in various contexts in his books, but often in an off-puttingly dry or theoretical way.

Extensive sections on the elements of the Enneagram are also to be found in Gurdjieff's chief work *Beelzebub's Tales To His Grandson* (in chapters 39 and 40). However, this work remained inaccessible to a wider public because of Gurdjieff's use of invented words. Bennett's Enneagram book was published in a very limited edition by Coombe Springs Press, the publishing house of Bennett's Sherborne House Institute in Gloucestershire (Academy for Continuous Education). It printed the lectures which Bennett gave regularly from 1971 until his death, for the use of his students.

Bennett's Enneagram book is still passed around rather secretly amongst Gurdjieff pupils. I am particularly fascinated by the title page of the first edition: between angel and devil we see a human being contained within an Enneagram, in the company of a lion, a bull and an eagle – the four figures of the Apocalypse. The drawing was made under Gurdjieff's direction in Tiflis in 1919, and was intended to be used for the 1923 programme of his Fontainebleau institute. It is possible that meditating on this fascinating drawing would reveal more about the content of the Enneagram than any book.

In spite of Bennett's book, the 'diagram of all life' – as the Enneagram was known in Gurdjieff circles – remained largely unknown. It was still practically impossible to understand Bennett's descriptions or Ouspensky's indications without the guidance of a teacher.

It is not generally known, either, that the Hindu writer and yoga philosopher Sri Aurobindo (Aurobindo Ghose), who lived

Figure 2   *The dust-jacket design for Bennett's Enneagram book*

from 1872 to 1950, also studied the Enneagram. It is not clear, though, whether he heard about it during his student days in England, or whether visionary insight gave him access to it. He might also have heard about the Enneagram from Ouspensky, who visited him in 1914 in Pondicherry in southern India.

Aurobindo inspired the American astrologer Patrizia Norelli-Bachelet to develop an 'astrology of the gnostic circle' based on the Enneagram; in the mid-seventies she published a clever but almost unreadable book on the subject.[3] It was difficult to get hold of either in America or Germany, and was soon forgotten.

Figure 3 *Original sketch for the 1923 programme of the Institute for the Harmonious Development of Man. The drawing was made in Tiflis in 1919 by Alexander de Salzmann*

A similar approach was made by Wilhelmine and Arnold Graf Keyserling in their philosophy of the WHEEL,[4] which never became known beyond their group of pupils in Vienna.

It was quite different in the case of the Indian master Bhagwan

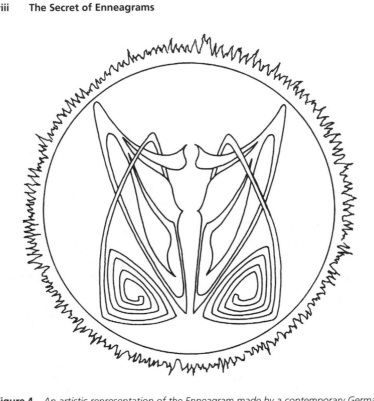

Figure 4   *An artistic representation of the Enneagram made by a contemporary German working group in Wiesbaden*

Rajneesh (Osho), who was a great devotee of Gurdjieff. Rajneesh considered Gurdjieff to be the only master of modern times teaching in Europe. At his ashram in Oregon, USA, he named a dam after Gurdjieff; there was also an 'Ouspensky Avenue' in the small village of the ashram. In the meeting room in Rajneesh's Indian ashram in Poona, a large Enneagram hung. His numerous pupils therefore became aware of this cosmic diagram, but without studying its source.

After Gurdjieff's death, the various separate groups led by Ouspensky and Bennett did not make a very good or united impression; they were riven by dispute about who truly represented the master's teachings, and who were his true successors.

The sum of Gurdjieff's legacy therefore seems to be a small number of active groups, several difficult books by Gurdjieff, Bennett and Ouspensky, and the visible symbol of the Enneagram. It is the aim of this present book to render the Enneagram of concrete and practical use in the business of living.

The Enneagram as a teaching of psychological types

Nowadays the most widely known, and very pragmatic Enneagram school, is based on the work of the Bolivian psychologist Oscar Ichazo. In 1968 he founded the Arica School (Instituto de Gnoselogia) in Chile, after studying the esoteric and mystical schools of both East and West for 15 years. Ichazo says that his teacher in La Paz, Bolivia, introduced him to the Sufi tradition of Enneagram work; but he has never revealed his name.

In 1971 Ichazo started the Arica School in New York (ARICA Institute Inc.), which became the source for many modern therapies. The Enneagram teaching found its way from here to the Esalen Institute in California, where it was a closely guarded secret until the end of the seventies. The Jesuits got to know about it there, and came to play a leading role in developing the Enneagram's psychological applications. From the mid-eighties onwards, such Ichazo-inspired Enneagram work fast became a therapeutic fashion, which made its way to Germany in 1988-9. In the process, though, the Enneagram unfortunately quickly became nothing more than a practical diagnostic typology.

Some Jesuits, particularly their organization of lay members, the 'Communities of Christian Life' (Gemeinschaften Christlicher Lebens – GCL) used the Enneagram in Germany as part of their spiritual discipline; and in the spring of 1989 the first German Enneagram conference took place at Schloss Craheim in Lower Franconia. So many people had, by then, developed an interest in the Enneagram teaching that the first 'Ecumenical Enneagram Study Group' was formed, whose aim was to prepare and organize conferences, workshops and meditations on the Enneagram.

Ichazo declared that he had been initiated into the Enneagram by Sufi teachers of Afghanistan. Gurdjieff and Bennett also had close links with certain Sufi orders – particularly the Sarmoun and the Naqshbandi Brotherhoods. Yet the two approaches to the Enneagram propounded by Gurdjieff and Ichazo are quite different from one another. Gurdjieff looked upon the Enneagram in terms of *movement, dynamics* and *process*. He connected it, as I have mentioned, with certain movement sequences; the theatre director Peter Brook gave a short impression of this at the end of his film about Gurdjieff.[5] Ouspensky throws some light on a dynamic approach to the Enneagram when he writes:

The Enneagram is continuous motion, the same perpetuum mobile that people have sought since time immemorial and failed to find. And it is clear why they cannot find it: they were seeking outside of themselves for something that was within them; and they tried to construct perpetual motion in the same way that a machine is constructed. But real continuous movement is a part of other motion and cannot be produced separately from it [. . .] To understand the Enneagram, one must imagine it in movement. An Enneagram that is not in motion is a dead symbol; a living symbol is in movement.[6]

The Enneagram should really be visualized in a three-dimensional form: the nine points on its periphery should be imagined as if distributed at certain intervals on a spiral. The Bohrs model of the atom may help us in forming a picture of this three-dimensional Enneagram.

Seen in this way, the Enneagram can be a comprehensive summation of all knowledge – and every piece of knowledge can be interpreted by means of it. Ouspensky, like Gurdjieff and Bennett, thought that only what you can embody in the Enneagram is knowledge you really possess.

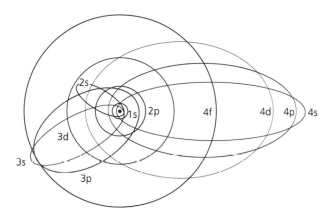

Figure 5   *The Bohrs model of the atom*

In contrast to this dynamic model, the Jesuits and the humanistic psychologists who base their work on Ichazo use the Enneagram in a static form: they see its separate peripheral points as part of a fixed sequence. This interpretation leads to a handy psychological typology, such as has been developed in easily accessible ways by Rohr and Ebert,[7] Riso[8] and Jaxon-Bear.[9]

In Gurdjieff's dynamic model, on the other hand, there is no fixed sequence of Enneagram points. Their position and relationship can alter from situation to situation, and depends largely on one's state of consciousness and particular interests and approach. The Gurdjieffian use of the Enneagram applies it to the dynamics of social situations, and to patterns of movement extending from the cosmos down to the microcosm of individual cells. Gurdjieff, Ouspensky and Bennett do not hold with the idea of fixed types of human beings. Every person is, rather, seen as a conglomeration of different egos – one of which, at any particular time and situation, will take control. There is, in this view, a continual alternation of personalities, unless the individual works upon herself with the help of a teacher versed in a proven tradition of self-development.

Although the Enneagram as propounded by Ichazo has become, since the eighties in America and since 1989 in

Germany, a familiar concept in esoteric circles, I haven't seen a single dictionary of symbols which refers to it. In spite of many efforts, the Enneagram still remains a blank patch on the esoteric map. This book aims to clarify the contours which this difficult concept conceals; also to show the practical benefits which Enneagram work can have.

Notes

1   Also known as the 'path of the shrewd person'. On this path, in contrast to that of the fakir, monk or yogi, one does not need to withdraw from the world. The Fourth Way also asserts the importance of simultaneously and harmoniously developing body, intellect and feeling. A fundamental tenet of this path is that the pupil may only do the things which he also understands. For more about this, see also: Ouspensky, P D, *The Fourth Way. A Record of Talks and Answers to Questions.*

   There are speculations, although not proved, that the builders of the Mont St Michel monastery, the early Quakers, and the Russian Freemasons were all pupils of the Fourth Way. The Knights Templar and the alchemists were also supposed to have been influenced by the (wandering) schools of the Fourth Way.

2   Bennett, John G, *The Enneagram*, (out of print). A new edition: *Enneagram Studies*, is still available in both Britain and the USA.

3   Norelli-Bachelet, Patrizia, *The Gnostic Circle: a synthesis.*

4   Interesting information about the WHEEL is provided by the following book, Neue Wiener Schule, *Im Jahr des Uranus. Der Weg des philosophischen Handwerks.* This contains the relevant essays by Wilhelmine and Arnold Keyserling.

5   Peter Brooks film of Gurdjieff's autobiography, *Meetings with Remarkable Men.* The last ten minutes of this film show one of the few existing film-sequences of the 'movements'.

6   Ouspensky, Piotr D, *In Search of the Miraculous.* This was the first book, in the West, to describe the teachings of Gurdjieff and the Enneagram.

7   Rohr, Richard and Ebert, Andreas. *Discovering the Enneagram. An ancient tool, a new spiritual journey.*

8   Riso, Richard, *Personality Types: Using the Enneagram for Self-Discovery.*

9   Jaxon-Bear, Eli: *Die neun Zahlen des Lebens. Das Enneagramm – Charakterfixierung und spirituelles Wachstum.*

CHAPTER 1

A Practical Tool for Life

> Intelligence is wholly naïve and has no concept that there are in fact 'proven methods' for doing things. Understanding is too slow and too alien to be of any great help. [. . .] For this reason intelligence is cheerful.
>
> *Anthony G E Blake*

Every completed process and every occurrence that is in motion (or should be) can be grasped with the help of the Enneagram: the growth of a plant, for example; also personal development, or the development of a project or of a group. The Enneagram perspective also helps to bring a process to completion. If I have got stuck in my personal development, or my business is not successful, or my house-plant does not seem healthy, the Enneagram can help me see where and why a process is blocked. So it is applicable to all life processes. You can use it to understand organizations, institutions and production processes; it is also an excellent tool for gaining deeper insight into your own actions and relationships. Wherever process-orientated thinking is required, consulting the Enneagram can help, for it shows how each step and point are part of a larger context. It sharpens our total awareness and can often reveal to us the factors determining our actions, and their consequences, which we would otherwise be unclear about.

Although when we begin an action we often know what its aim is, we very rarely foresee the circumstances we will encounter on the way. In the planning of larger projects in particular, we tend to overlook the nitty-gritty details of the path towards our goal. In the case of our own relationships and actions, we all have a tendency to 'blind spots', or, as depth-psychology would put it, to suppress things.

Changing ourselves

I would like to demonstrate the usefulness of the Enneagram with an example taken from actual everyday life. In case you are wondering how I have determined and assigned the individual Enneagram points, turn to chapter 3. But it is better, I think, to ponder these concrete examples before getting to grips with theoretical considerations. We all know situations in which we feel unhappy with ourselves and our own lives. We all long to be content and fulfilled. Let us look at such a situation in terms of the Enneagram illustrated opposite.

The process of change begins at *Enneagram point 1*, where I become aware of being unhappy. This unhappiness creates a conflict, which drives me to action. I may decide to alter my situation fundamentally, thus entering into the process model of the Enneagram. Standing at point 1, I can look along the line towards point 7, and see an aspect of the goal I strive for.

What the work stimulated by my unhappiness really means, is still not clear to me at this initial point; but at least I know that I must change my present state. The tension between my present feeling of unhappiness and my goal of happiness shows me point 4 of the Enneagram. At point 4 I am compelled to confront my own defence mechanisms or resistance to change – it is often just pure laziness that I have to struggle with.

With my goal before me, and an inkling of the way I resist change, I begin to understand why I am so unhappy. I continually and mechanically repeat the same patterns of behaviour, which make me discontented or unhappy. This is Sigmund Freud's definition of neurosis: a compulsive pattern which puts happiness beyond reach.

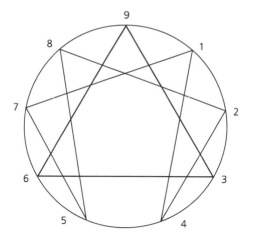

9 Love/higher consciousness

8 I attain my goal	1 I am unhappy
7 I serve the self-given goal	2 I become aware of repeating situations
6 I awaken	3 Something new enters my life
5 I begin to make use of the energy of conflict	4 I confront my defence mechanisms

Figure 6 *The challenge of unhappiness*

This knowledge allows me to advance to *Enneagram point 2*. Now I can get a clearer view of my aim, since Enneagram point 8 is in my sights.

However, my inner resistance (point 4) still puts the happiness I desire beyond my grasp. If I remain unable to open myself to something new – which comes from beyond myself and provides me with new, stirring impulses – I will stay unhappy and end up as a frustrated misery-guts.

In this condition I no longer know how things can continue; I am at the end of my tether. Looking at the Enneagram shows me immediately that I am now in urgent need of outside help. This can be in the form of a (spiritual) teacher, a book, a therapist or a group – something, anyway, that challenges me to face my own repeating patterns. Such an impetus from without – which can also take the form of some kind of shock, such as a separation, or losing a job – starts me in a new direction. In this self-development or therapy Enneagram, each point represents something that is required of me. At *Enneagram point 3d*, therefore, I must become active. I must seek out for myself the therapist, teacher, group or book which can help me overcome my mechanical habits. If someone leaves me or I lose my job, I will not derive any advantage from it until I actively react to the shock, to what has happened. It is very common at this point for people simply to wait for a teacher or some helpful angel to fall from the skies and save them; but this inevitably leads one back into the old repetitive patterns, back into the sleepwalking state. Yet the activity needed here is not usually of a very conscious, goal-orientated kind; rather it is an unconscious reaction which allows me to find, as though by chance, the impetus I need from without.

The spiritual tradition of the Sufis designates the condition of 'sleep' (and also 'blindness') as one in which we react particularly strongly to unimportant dimensions of life, so as to defend ourselves from the reality that *is* important for us. We refuse to see, for example, that we are undisciplined, lazy, addicted and completely dependent on our environment. Sleep is, ultimately, always a state of ego-possession. This is the illusion or deception, which, in the first Enneagram stage, always binds us in the – superficially not unpleasant – condition of sleep. The practice of self-remembering works against this.

Excursus: the practice of self-remembering

The Gurdjieff work[1] begins at the third Enneagram point with the practice of self-remembering and self-observation, which is usually shown one by a teacher in a group. Gurdjieff describes self-remembering as active, intentional and conscious contemplation, in the course of which one becomes self-aware. Real self-observation takes place in a fraction of a second, and affects us emotionally. You should not, ideally, write down the results of your self-observation or try to fix them by other means, since you would then easily succumb to the temptation to add something to the actual observation that did not truly belong to it.

Before a person begins to study this mechanicality and all principles of a properly guided self-observation, he must first make an irrevocable resolve to always want to be unequivocally honest with himself, to shut his eyes to nothing, to evade nothing that may result, wherever it may lead, to fear no consequences, and to not limit himself by previously determined boundaries [. . .] By means of properly conducted self-observation, a person will, from the very first days onwards, gain clear insight into, and indubitable recognition of, his complete powerlessness and helplessness in the face of literally everything which surrounds him.[2]

Let us take an example to make clear what distinguishes self-remembering or self-observation from our normal everyday way of living. As you read these lines, you can direct your attention to what I am saying. That is concentration. But you can also become aware of yourself as a reader and clearly sense yourself at the same time as you absorb information. You sense the reader in yourself . . . the following Buddhist story makes the process clearer.

A devotee of Buddha possessed a beautiful, precious and very old Buddha statue, which he prized greatly, and which he took with him on all his travels. On one journey, quite unexpectedly, he was suddenly overtaken by a snowstorm and sought refuge in a barn. After a while he felt so frozen that he was afraid he would die. He had already given up hope of surviving when the Buddha appeared to him and asked: 'Why don't you burn me?' The man was greatly frightened and vigorously rejected this idea. But the Buddha laughed and said: 'If you seek me in the statue you will never find me. I am not to be found in any object, I am in the one who worships. I am the one who is shivering in you. So burn this statue!'

The story shows that the idea of self-observation has a long history; it is not only found in Gurdjieff's system.

The Gurdjieff principle of self-observation requires us to use the surplus energies, which we do not need either for our own sustenance or unconsciously to serve a higher power, for the development of our own higher faculties. At the same time it is important neither to express negative feelings nor allow ourselves to be tempted into negative acts. It must be our aim to observe such processes neutrally, from a distance. Modern depth-psychology regards this approach in terms of a withdrawal from our own projections. This allows us to achieve an attitude of permanently conscious effort, and of intentional suffering, which arises because we oppose our own automatic patterns of behaviour.

But it must be stressed that passive suffering alone is of no use. We have to move on to a state of conscious and voluntary suffering. Our awareness replaces the purely mechanical identification with our own suffering with a conscious observation of its causes. We need to realize that our everyday feelings are anxiety-ridden because of the social context we are part of. They impede our objective view of reality and our actions. By minutely observing these feelings – without, initially, trying to change them – we do in fact change them and open ourselves to the real feelings which underlie them, although we will only experience their full, living reality from point 6 of the Enneagram onwards.

We can best stimulate the process of self-remembering by combatting any expression of negative feelings. Such feelings are always unconscious and therefore in opposition to conscious self-recollection. Energies become available to us when we refrain from the expression of negative feelings; and we can then use these in self-remembering. If, for example, we refrain from expressing rage about something, we can consciously use its energies to recognize how we arrived at this state; an exercise like this can reveal to us many unexpected things about ourselves.

You will also find that the state of self-remembering actually protects you from negative feelings. When you have reached this stage there will be nothing to stop you embarking on the Gurdjieff 'work' itself.

The 'work' consists, initially, of observing yourself systematically. It is my practice, for instance, to try to become conscious of myself every morning for about three to five minutes. As I do this, I try to look beyond what the Swiss depth-psychologist Carl Gustav Jung (1875–1961) called the 'persona' – in other words behind the mask which I present to the world. I observe the role which I cannot, unfortunately, stop playing. I am often shocked to find how many things I say and do which are quite contrary to my intentions. I try to be as honest as possible with myself.

During this practice of self-remembering, I remain aware of myself, although I also simultaneously perceive my environment. The first step is to sense continually how I receive impulses from my environment and process them. Anyone taking up this practice will initially only remember himself with his intellect, by saying inwardly: 'I sense myself', or 'I now remember myself'. But his aim must be to remember himself through his emotions, which happens by itself after practising for some time. What this really means will only become apparent to you when, during your self-remembering, you suddenly have a deep sense of yourself and become completely calm. It is Gurdjieff's view that this conscious composure in everyday life ultimately protects us against all wrong or evil. We will make far fewer errors in our everyday life if we remember ourselves frequently during the course of the day. At the end of the ballet, *The Struggle of the Magicians*, the white magicians pray:

> Creator God and all your helpers, help us to remember ourselves at all times, so that we may avoid unintentional actions, for it is only by means of these that evil can manifest.[3]

We can work towards this conscious attitude of self-remembering with the following exercise.

- Sit motionless on a hard chair.
- Rest your feet firmly on the ground, keep your eyes shut.
- Your head, neck and spine should form a straight line.
- Relax completely; let your shoulders drop loosely, and place your hands palm down on your upper thighs.

- Breathe in a deep, relaxed and regular fashion.
- Now try to concentrate on the feelings within your inner solar plexus, your heart and head, and to be fully present as you do so.

This exercise should be done every day before breakfast, for no longer than three minutes to begin with.

Once you have begun to remember yourself more easily, you can, in the morning when you take your first bite of food, and in the evening at sunset, try to be as intensely aware of yourself as possible. After a while this exercise develops your capacity to share your attention between yourself and your environment (as described at point 6 of the Enneagram). It is only then that you can fully and clearly recognize reality – which is the content of the exercise as well as of life itself.

To begin with it is particularly helpful to say to yourself while attempting this exercise: 'I am observing myself'. It is important to be fully aware of yourself during self-observation; to sense your body as intensively as possible. The first aim of this exercise is to gain insight into the fact that we actually never, or only very seldom, remember ourselves.

If you manage to remember yourself – even for the space of a few breaths – without being disturbed by any other thoughts, then you can extend this exercise to your everyday life. As you read this text, for instance, you can try to perceive your body. It is easiest to sense your right hand. Concentrate on the feeling in your right hand, and continue reading, at the same time saying to yourself: 'I am reading'. By doing this all your feelings will come to a standstill. You will read with a high degree of consciousness; the impression made on you by what you read will be stronger, and you will retain the information for longer. You can apply this approach to every kind of work.

In the advanced form of self-remembering, our attention is divided between being aware of our body and of what we are presently doing or perceiving. Self-perception in ordinary every-day life is divided between the ego and the observed object.

Neither self-remembering nor self-observation are encouraged in our society. That is why we often lack the ability and motivation for achieving it. You can overcome inner resistance by making a firm decision to relax and sense your body from within, for at least three minutes each day. Train your attention like a muscle, sending it into the inside of your body.

Self remembering, which is an intense form of self-observation, helps you to stop reacting automatically. It is a process which begins by getting to know yourself better and becoming more aware of yourself.

One of the first effects of conscious self-remembering is the (painful) realization that you possess no will-power or self-discipline. You should be clear, though, that regular self-remembering will enable you to create the conditions in which your will can slowly develop. It requires deep insight to see through the illusion that you possess a self-determining will. You can support the self-remembering exercise by stopping whatever you are doing, at least once a day, and becoming aware which centre within you is at work, and in which way. You will find that your intellectual centre relates to your environment by comparing two or more impressions; your emotional centre evaluates whether something is pleasant or unpleasant to you; and your movement centre shows a particularly high speed of reactive capacity. Try to notice whether or not your centres are working for you in the most suitable way. Is your feeling centre, for instance, appropriating the role of rational decision?

A variation of the self-remembering exercise is to speak aloud the word 'I', and then observe carefully in which centre within you this word resounds. After some practice, you can try to transpose the vibrations of this word 'I' from one centre to another.

The opposite of self-remembering is identification. When we identify with something, our attention is focused only upon it, and we no longer have a sense of ourselves. We then become prey to factors in our surroundings, which toss us hither and thither like a plaything. This is why identification with the other in a relationship is so dangerous; by identifying we lose ourselves.

At Enneagram points 1 and 2 (sometimes also 3 and 4), we are liable to identify ourselves with our work, personality, social position or even our suffering. This identification robs us of the energy which we need for self-remembering, and imprisons us in the situation in which we presently find ourselves.

After this – quite important – digression, let us return to the process of self-change we were examining with the help of the Enneagram points.

I am still at *Enneagram point 3*. There are many paths I can take here. What is important is to realize that I must be active in some way at this point if I am to overcome unhappiness. Sometimes it is necessary at this stage to change environment and friends. I may have to move somewhere new, begin again in some way – at any rate strive towards the new and unknown (which often takes the shape of things that one is particularly afraid of).

Once I have really taken this on board, I have, metaphorically speaking, found my 'cure', and moved on to *Enneagram point 4*. At this stage I will inevitably encounter enormous inner tensions but this is still the path *I* have chosen.

Knowing about these tensions in advance is beneficial, for it helps me bear them. They derive ultimately from the old, entrenched habits which appear from undercover hiding places, and use all their power to do battle with my attempts to change. Superficially these habits seem like laziness. They can easily lead me to look upon the exercises I undertake as a banal waste of time, as ridiculous esoteric hocus-pocus. I may decide to break off my therapy, mistrusting therapists and teachers and believing that there are far more profitable ways of spending my time. If I have come to the end of a relationship, I may immediately – more or less consciously – seek a new partner with whom I fall head over heels in love. I convince myself that I am in love; and sooner or later will find myself back in the old pattern of discontent.

This is exactly what the Enneagram shows. Look at it carefully: it is quite in the order of things to expect a crisis at Enneagram point 4. The danger of slipping back into old automatic behaviour is very great at this stage. The Enneagram point 4 connects back to points 1 and 2; this means that one has the tendency at this stage to look at the past through rose-tinted spectacles, and so to flee from new tension and conflict, taking refuge in old patterns.

The Enneagram teaches us that we can make productive use of these tensions that we resist, for they allow something new to arise in us – they change us and make it possible for us to restructure ourselves in both psychic and physical ways.

In spite of all resistance, I have the feeling at Enneagram point 4 that my own efforts have an effect. This helps me work further towards attaining a goal.

By living through these tensions, and bearing them, I can progress to *Enneagram point 5*. After all the doubt and conflict at point 4, the liberation I desired is unfortunately still not available. Yet an important step has been taken; for at point 5 I clearly recognize the attitudes and behaviour which really make me content. My goal – Enneagram points 7 and 8 – is in my sights. On the one hand I therefore find it easier to use my inner tensions; on the other hand, though, perceiving the desired goal yet being unable to reach it, causes me pain.

Enneagram point 5 teaches me that I must accept conscious suffering if I am to come closer to my goal. In my inner struggle, and by living in the tension between yes and no, I can change myself. Protracted conscious suffering breaks down the programming in which I am trapped and allows me to shed my ideas and fantasies about myself, and my attraction to an easy, comfortable life.

Just as at Enneagram point 3, I need an outer stimulus to move on from this stage. This outer impetus occurs at *Enneagram point 6*. At this point I grasp everything which I have experienced up to now. I succeed in finally switching off the automatic reactions that I have struggled with for so long. According to Gurdjieff, body and psyche have now finally restructured themselves. I awake from sleep and now no longer react accidentally and automatically to all outer influences, like a leaf in the wind. The various personalities that struggle with each other within me in an anarchic fashion no longer respond in a chaotic way to all sorts of outer impulses, and so I am spared the inner conflicts that previously plagued me. By enduring these tensions, a coherent ego has been created within me that possesses a goal-orientated will. Previously, every ego within me had its own particular will; now I become able to unite these behind one single will. Only now can I really act in a coherent way. Formerly I dreamed or 'freely associated', and called this process 'thinking'. The 'will' was for me just a vague result of wish and desire. Now I can begin to understand that the will depends upon a very conscious form of existence, which requires my determined and applied effort.

The moment has now come when an outer impetus is needed. For this a therapist, a teacher or at least a book is required, to mediate the necessary insights; very occasionally a sympathetic friend or partner can assume this role.

In the 'work', I now manage, after practising self-remembering (Enneagram point 3), to turn my attention both towards myself and my environment. I am no longer focused on myself and the feelings within me alone, but find the will simultaneously to exist in two centres at once: in myself and in the outer world. This division of attention is connected with overcoming the ego. I no longer feel myself as the centre of the world, but can recognize outer, objective reality. Depth-psychologists regard this phenomenon as the withdrawal of projection. Both C G Jung and his colleague Erich Neumann (1905–1960) saw this division of attention as an overcoming of 'fascination': I am no longer under the spell of either myself or something outside myself; I am not oblivious of myself, but experience myself as integrated in a real and living way with my environment.

At Enneagram point 6, therefore, I wake up – I win my battle with sleep and overcome my unhappiness. From now on I am no longer at the mercy of neurotic and unproductive repetitions.

I have, in fact, arrived at *Enneagram point 7*; it is here that I can begin to serve my goal or task with all my strength. In our example, I manage to focus all my energy on my happiness. By doing so I reach *Enneagram point 8*, where I attain my aim. At this stage I can clearly recognize my automatic mechanisms as the source of my unhappiness (Enneagram point 2). I also understand how important it was to make positive and productive use of my conflicts (Enneagram point 5).

At *Enneagram point 9*, I am free to enter upon a new process of development with an enhanced and altered consciousness. Enneagram point 9 always seems connected in some way with love. Gurdjieff distinguished three kinds of love:

- Purely physical love as sexual attraction
- Emotional love, which often tends to transform itself into hate
- Conscious love, which leads to the perfection of both partners

At Enneagram point 9, it is the third form of love that is active. This point symbolizes the higher being that has been at work within us throughout, giving us the energy to endure and pass on through this often very arduous process.

Body, spirit, soul – the integrated development of the human being

The concept 'soul' is used here in the sense C G Jung used it. For Jung the soul was a person's specific relationship to his unconscious. For me, it is the living feeling within a person. Gurdjieff's concept of the soul was only superficially different: he considered that the human being is not naturally endowed with soul but that he must first earn and attain it.

All religions are rooted in the idea that the human being possesses a soul, while atheism categorically rejects this. Emma Jung and Marie-Louise von Franz[4] interpret the Grail legend, which so preoccupied the people of the Middle Ages, in the Gurdjieffian sense as a development of soul within oneself, similar to the alchemists who sought the soul within matter. Attaining soulhood was *the* problem of the Middle Ages. According to C G Jung, this is an attempt to realize the anima, to form the soul which is not yet perfect and complete in the human being but is present only as potential; and which can be created and formed through particular processes, which the Enneagram represents.

In the literature on Gurdjieff and the Enneagram one often encounters the – historically false – opinion that Gurdjieff was the first to teach that we must develop soul. There are clear parallels between Jung and Gurdjieff in this respect, which are perhaps partly explained by the fact that pupils of Jung, such as Maurice Nicholl, became closely involved with Gurdjieff – to the dismay of Jung himself.

The Enneagram makes clear that significant changes in personality always involve body, feeling (soul) and intellect (spirit or mind). I first experience myself as a human being with a body that has been born into the world. This body is living and allows me to move. As such, I am at *Enneagram point 1*, and recognize that this living body is the prerequisite for recognizing my feelings (Enneagram point 4) and intellectually understanding myself and my environment (Enneagram point 7).

At *Enneagram point 2*, I have to keep my body healthy and train it in order to retain its vitality. I make efforts to stay healthy and mobile in order to attain a freedom that is still unknown to me (Enneagram point 8) and in order to get in touch with my feelings (Enneagram point 4).

This Enneagram shows clearly that neither spirit nor intellect can attain freedom without the body. I will also never perceive and truly recognize my feelings if I do not preserve my body's vitality and flexibility. As Wilhelm Reich (1897–1957), a pupil of Freud recognized, only crippled feelings live in a stagnating, inflexible body.

But however much I train my body, at some point – in fact at *Enneagram point 3* – I will realize with a shock that something else is at work within me, that draws attention to itself through moods and feelings, and that cannot be dealt with simply by cold showers or disregard.

At *Enneagram point 4*, I come into relationship with my

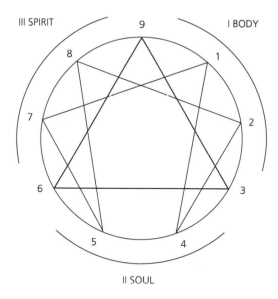

III SPIRIT   9   I BODY

II SOUL

9   The wholly integrated human being (The fully evolved individual)

8 I attain freedom	1 My body is flexible
7 I understand myself and my environment	2 I work to keep my body healthy
6 Spirit (intellect)	3 Psyche (feeling)
5 I try to consciously influence my feeelings	4 I strive to perceive my feelings

Figure 7   *The body-soul-spirit Enneagram*

feelings and try to recognize, grasp and understand them. But this effort throws me back upon my body. I experience my dependency on drives, desires and mood swings that arise from my bodily condition (Enneagram points 1 and 2). But it also dawns on me that these do not represent the whole world of my feelings. I begin to attempt to influence my feelings by means of my will, so as not to remain the slave of moods and drives my whole life long. Now I am at *Enneagram point 5*, and see that in order to truly understand myself and to attain freedom, a new quality must enter into the process.

At *Enneagram point 6*, I discover the power of spirit or intellect, and thus begin to understand myself and my environment at a new level.

Enneagram points 7 and 8 show me that body, soul and spirit are all necessary for the attainment of freedom. I only understand myself and my environment (Enneagram point 7) when my body is flexible (Enneagram point 1) and when I am, at the same time, master of my feelings (Enneagram point 5). I attain freedom (Enneagram point 8) when I have mastered my feelings (Enneagram point 5) and my body (Enneagram point 2).

In my Gurdjieff group, Gurdjieff's metaphor of the coach and horses is very popular as a description of the connection between body, soul and spirit: the coach corresponds to our physical body; the harnessed horses correspond to the feelings, and the coachman to the controlling force of intellect. In the coach sits the Lord/Lady and Master/Mistress (the true ego, according to Gurdjieff), who decides where the coach is going. When we arrive at Enneagram point 8, we direct the intellect (the coach driver) where to go, so that it can control our feelings (the horses), and so that the coach (the body) arrives at the desired place. Until Enneagram point 6, the Lord/Lady and Master/Mistress is absent, and there is no one to say in which direction the coach should go. Such a journey often ends in the ditch, since the coach driver intellect is usually asleep and, until Enneagram point 4 at least, the horses (feelings) just bolt.

If you want to apply the Enneagram to yourself or others, it is very helpful to keep this simile in mind.

The dynamic between body, soul and spirit represented in *figure 7*, is just one way of viewing your own development in the Enneagram mirror. If you are more intellectually orientated, then the Enneagram points corresponding to the intellect (7 and 8 in *figure 7*) take the place of the Enneagram points relating to the body (1 and 2 in *figure 7*). If, in addition, you are closer to your body than to your feelings, the Enneagram points relating to the body (1 and 2 in *figure 7*) will follow. This form of schematic pattern corresponds to the male archetype. The female archetype orders the Enneagram points in the sequence: feeling, body, intellect.[5]

This example clearly shows how the appropriate allocation of qualities to the Enneagram points depends on a particular situation and approach.

It is possible to imagine a further Enneagram, in which

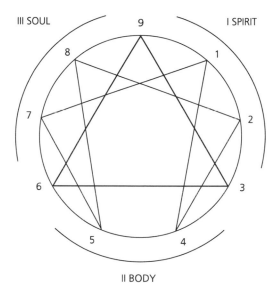

III SOUL   9   I SPIRIT

II BODY

9 Beyond male or female

8 Through a combined, constructive application of feelings, body and intellect, I attain freedom

7 I experience my feelings in their dependency upon body and intellect

6 Psyche (feeling)

5 I begin to make creative use of my bodily tensions and to consciously influence them

1 I have a (flexible) intellect

2 I train my intellect (apply it)

3 Body

4 I strive to keep my body flexible and perceive its needs (struggle against laziness)

Figure 8   *The male archetype in the Enneagram*

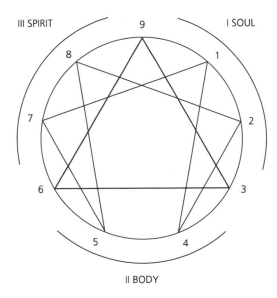

III SPIRIT   9   I SOUL

II BODY

9   Beyond male or female

8   I can use my will to make use of my
    feelings and my body for spiritual goals
7   I understand my body and my feelings
6   Spirit (intellect)
5   I begin to make creative use of my
    bodily tensions and to influence my
    body through my conscious will

1   I sense my feelings
2   I become aware of the way I express my
    feelings
3   Body
4   I try to keep my body attractive and
    flexible and to perceive its needs
    (struggle against laziness and
    role-playing)

Figure 9   *The female archetype in the Enneagram*

points 1 and 2 are allocated to the feeling realm, points 4 and 5 to the intellectual realm and points 7 and 8 to the body. You may like to draw this Enneagram yourself and try to understand its dynamic and relate it to yourself.

If we use the Enneagram for practical self-knowledge and help in determining our actions, it draws our attention to the following patterns and laws, which we otherwise easily overlook, suppress or even reject.

- I must clarify my material conditions or my outer situation before I am ready for purposeful and goal-orientated actions. I must become aware of my present situation and standpoint (Enneagram point 1).
- I must become active and be prepared to open myself to outside help (Enneagram point 2).
- When I have become conscious of my automatic reactions, and have opened myself to helpful impulses from without, I am confronted by inner conflicts (Enneagram point 3).
- A creative solution can only come about when I endure these conflicts and do not fall back into my old, automatic ways of reacting (sleep!). If I cannot manage this, I succumb to a vicious circle: I advance from Enneagram point 1 to Enneagram point 4, but then, because of the apparently unbearable conflicts I am exposed to, or because of laziness, I take refuge once more in old patterns of behaviour and end up at Enneagram point 1 again. If I do not develop the discipline to break through this vicious circle and endure my conflicts, I will never be able to move on from the right side of the Enneagram to the left.
- The emotional conflicts and tensions at Enneagram points 4 and 5, open me up to fundamentally new potential. I must find the courage to allow myself to be touched by the unknown and drawn towards it. I must give myself to it. The conflict ultimately gives me access to intuition or the inner voice.
- From Enneagram point 6 onwards, I no longer suffer from my contradictory feelings, unclarified motives and inability to take decisions (which are caused by my competing egos). My many egos are welded into one through the hammer of conflict.[6] The alchemists called this condition the *Transmutatio*, which means that what was previously available as potential has been transformed into reality.[7] To put it in simpler terms: the possibilities for transforming yourself into an individual with a consciously directed will, which formed at Enneagram points 4 and 5 through inner conflicts, now becomes reality.

The analysis of work processes

Practical application of the Enneagram is not confined to developing self-knowledge; it can also successfully be used in clarifying production and work processes. One example is the writing of this book.

The first, material, consideration for writing this book, consists of a medium for composing the text (*Enneagram point 1*). This medium needs to be structured in such a way as to enable the relevant ideas to be composed and presented (Enneagram

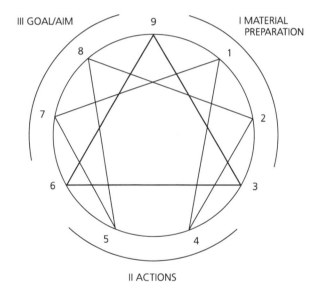

9   You have ideas about another book

8   The book is read
7   The book is published
6   Publisher
5   The idea is used to order and communicate the available material

1   The computer is operating a text software programme
2   The relevant books are read, and experience gathered
3   Idea
4   The search for a form in which the material can be presented

Figure 10   *Writing the Enneagram book*

point 4). In this case, a computer is needed that has both text and graphics capabilities. In addition, the text format must be of such a nature as to facilitate its use as a basis for publication. The computer programmes used must therefore be compatible with the publisher's own system (Enneagram point 7).

Once these basic requirements are met, the author must have practical knowledge and experience of the Enneagram, and have gathered as much information as possible on relevant themes (*Enneagram point 2*). The knowledge gained through my own experiences, and the knowledge of other authors on the same theme, provides the necessary preconditions for the development of an idea. At Enneagram point 4 I must become clear what exactly it is that I wish to communicate through this book. It is important to be aware of other books on the same theme, since they may inform the expectations of the reader (Enneagram point 8). As author I need to be able to judge what the reader is likely to know and what he is not likely to know. In concrete terms in this case, I cannot assume that the readers of this book are familiar either with experiences in Gurdjieff groups or with Gurdjieff exercises.

But all these preconditions are not yet material enough for the writing of a book. I need the attentions of the famous Muse, who inspires me with an idea (*Enneagram point 3*). The idea must also be acceptable to the publisher (Enneagram point 6). The idea for this book came to me in conversation with my editor, who assumed the role of Muse and midwife.

Once I had the idea of writing a book about the Enneagram, I had to find ways of presenting the available material (*Enneagram point 4*). For this I needed a knowledge of the Enneagram books based on the work of Oscar Ichazo, since I wished to exclude from this book his Enneagram-based typology. I also did not want to give much space to the Christian-Jesuit approach to the Enneagram, even though the work of Ouspensky – and also, to some extent, of Gurdjieff himself – was rooted in a deep Christian tradition. Instead, my focus in this book was to be my own experiences with the teachings of Gurdjieff, Ouspensky and especially Bennett (Enneagram point 2). Thus I set limits to the theme and material. My computer would be quite capable of making diagrammatic representions of the Enneagram (Enneagram point 1).

At *Enneagram point 5*, the most difficult task in this process awaited me – to plan a structure, and therefore also a list of contents and Enneagrams for the book. My plan for the organization of my material had to take into account the fact that the book would be published by Goldmann Verlag. It would therefore need to correspond with this publisher's requirements (Enneagram point 7). The form that suggested itself was that of an esoteric handbook, which would be both rich in content and easily accessible.

The final stage is for the book to appeal to my readers – which I hope is the case! (Enneagram point 8). I struggled for a long time trying to decide whether I should start with concrete examples and then proceed to a general explanation of the Enneagram (inductive method) or vice versa (deductive). Thinking of you, the reader, it seemed to me that the inductive approach would be more interesting and accessible. It also corresponds better with the nature of the Enneagram, which always refers to very concrete situations, projects or processes.

At *Enneagram point 6*, the publisher got involved in the process. At this point the length and scope of the book, the form of illustrations, and contractual considerations were decided. (*Enneagram point 7*).

Once I had made an analysis of the desired process with help of the Enneagram, the actual realization of it posed no problem. I could just stick to the procedure already mapped out.

You now have this book in your hand, and thus are at *Enneagram point 8* of the process. If you have read up to this point and will continue to read further the goal of my work has been achieved. As a result, you will ultimately be able to apply the Enneagram to your own work – which one could see as *Enneagram point 9*.

The American industrialist Henry Ford (1863–1947) is supposed to have used the Enneagram as a help in introducing the conveyor belt method of production. I don't know exactly how he went about applying the Enneagram to the problem of rationalizing the car industry to manufacture a cheap, mass-produced vehicle. But I can sketch out my idea of how it might have happened. You could also try it yourself, making an exact study of the connecting lines of the Enneagram model. The exciting thing about using the Enneagram is that there are often many different creative solutions to a problem. Here, anyway, is my suggestion:

I MATERIAL PRECONDITIONS
1 Raw materials are available
2 Factory and labour force exist
3 Now a production idea is needed: the car

II CONSIDERATIONS ABOUT THE PRODUCT
4 The idea is to produce as many cars as possible
5 This suggests the wholly new idea of serially produced cars
6 Car manufacture therefore needs to be rationalized

III PRODUCTION
7 The conveyor belt is introduced
8 The production process becomes more profitable and the product cheaper; the turnover therefore increases and production becomes still more profitable
9 The cheap, mass-produced car is born. A new era of individual mass transport begins

This is one way that Henry Ford and his son Edsel might have gone about it. This example shows, at least, that using the Enneagram in the rationalization of production processes can lead to new kinds of practical solutions. In the seventies, one of Bennett's pupils, Tony Hodgson, recognized this fact, and after Bennett's death founded the magazine *Systematics* (published by Coombe Springs Press) to promote the use of the Enneagram in the management of modern industry.

Practical use

These examples of the Enneagram's practical use clearly show:

1   That the practical application of the Enneagram develops an integrated, holistic view of complex structures. Factors determining situations become transparent; one's own standpoint and its limited perspective becomes clear. It is good, therefore, to use the Enneagram as often as possible. Not only will your eyes then be opened to new, undreamed-of possibilities, but you will also be able to view and grasp even complex sets of circumstances quicker and more precisely.

2   That the Enneagram shows clearly which steps in a process must be taken and when, and on what they depend. It marks out the path by which a problem can be solved in a conscious and focused way. It will certainly be useful to you to draw up an Enneagram before embarking on larger projects whose ramifications are hard to foresee; this will show you the directions and sequences which need to be followed.

3   At what stage one currently is in a process, what aspects need to be taken into account, and what challenges one is likely to encounter; also, why one is not making any progress, or just going round in circles.

In spite of the enormous usefulness of the Enneagram, a warning must be given: the Enneagram should not be grasped with the intellect alone. *Figures 7, 8* and *9* clearly demonstrate that knowledge is always dependent on the harmonious integration of body, soul and mind. Allow the Enneagram to affect all aspects of you; allow yourself to be challenged! Paint it, give it artistic form. Get to grips with it by going beyond the confines of the intellect. When you are at the beach, for instance, you can perhaps draw a large Enneagram in the sand and walk along its lines. In Bennett's institute at Sherborne House, there was a rose garden in the form of an Enneagram; by walking along the paths, people could experience its dynamics through the senses.

Such things will help you in your practical work with the Enneagram, helping you to understand it better and better.

This book is capable only of providing outer knowledge about the Enneagram. I would also like to encourage you to develop an inner understanding of it, which represents the highest stage of its practical application.

Notes

1   The rather off-putting term 'work' is used here and in the rest of the book in the sense in which it was employed in Gurdjieff groups. It expresses the striving to become conscious of oneself and one's environment. This 'work' is, according to Gurdjieff, intimately connected with clearly designated exercises and group interaction. This term – a typical Gurdjieff abbreviation – which embodied the concept of activities and learning within a Gurdjieff group, was conceived by Gurdjieff himself in 1916, in his St Petersburg group.

2   Gurdjieff, G I, *Beelzebub's Tales To His Grandson*, Vol. 3.

3   Cited in: Moore, James, *Gurdjieff. The Anatomy of a Myth. A Biography*, page 147. As well as this informative biography by an experienced activist in Gurdjieff groups, see also: Gurdjieff, G I: *The Struggle of the Magicians*. This book contains the original text of the ballet, but is extremely hard to get hold of.

4   Jung, Emma, and von Franz, Marie-Louise, *Grail Legend*; Jung, C G: *Psychology and Alchemy*.

5   I am sure I don't need to emphasize that these archetypes are just ideal and typical tendencies, and don't encompass 'man' and 'woman' as such. Both male and female archetypes are to be found in both men and women. When one works towards self-perfection with the help of the Enneagram, one ultimately combines both male and female archetypes as a unity within oneself. One arrives at what Jung, echoing the alchemists of the Middle Ages, called *Coniunctio* or the birth of the complete human being.

6   Alchemy speaks of an 'inner fire in the blood', whose heat produces a welding process. At Enneagram points 4 and 5 one can clearly experience such inner fire in one's feelings. It is important not to extinguish this fire too soon through the coldness of the intellect, otherwise the unifying process will not occur. Rationalization has a destructive tendency which immediately catapults us out of the process and leaves us paralysed again in the old, automatic routine.

7   Alchemy would see the Enneagram as the 'Philosophers' Stone', which is what it was also called by Gurdjieff.

CHAPTER 2

The History of the Enneagram

What seems pure 'chance' can be the veil behind which is hidden a concealed intention of the mind.

Anthony G E Blake

Many readers may be interested to know the origin of the Enneagram, and the cultural context it came from. But historical observations should not ignore the fact that in different epochs people have perceived it in quite different ways. Today, at the end of the 20th century, we are influenced by chaos theory and the implications of artificial intelligence; and the Enneagram therefore represents something different to us than it would have done to a brotherhood of the 10th century.

The Sarmoun Brotherhood

Gurdjieff claimed in his autobiographical novel, *Meetings with Remarkable Men*, that he had encountered the Enneagram amongst the Sarmoun Brotherhood in his many travels through the Middle East. However, the only reports of the existence of this brotherhood stem from Gurdjieff himself. The people in Gurdjieff's circles assumed that this secret brotherhood probably intentionally concealed its work (and perhaps still does), for otherwise its activities would have been commented on by numerous other travellers to the Middle East.

Bennett assumes that the wise Achaldan Community of Atlantis, which is often praised in *Beelzebub's Tales To His Grandson*, was a forerunner of the Sarmoun Brotherhood.

But if we look more closely at the episode in *Meetings with Remarkable Men*, in which Gurdjieff recounts how he came upon the first concrete signs of the Sarmoun Brotherhood, I believe it shows that we are dealing with a symbolic or metaphorical account. Gurdjieff wrote that in 1886 (at the age of 20), he discovered several old books which he took with him to Ani, the deserted former capital of Armenia, so that he could examine them in peace. Here he came upon an underground passage that led down to a collapsed monk's cell. It was there that he found old texts that told of the Sarmoun Brotherhood.

This underground passage and the old cell concealed deep below ground, seem to me to relate more to psychic than to physical geography. I see the discovery of the monk's cell as the Enneagram point 3, the first shock point – a psychic realm of the unconscious, from which the power of intuition arises. This becomes clearer still in the course of the story. Gurdjieff sought out the Brotherhood, and two or three years later was led to their chief temple. In his description, in which he is taken there in a highly dramatic way, wearing a blindfold, we find all sorts of indications of an esoteric topography: as in Scandinavian mythology he first crosses a dangerous bridge, also reminiscent of the Islamic idea of a bridge over hell, or of Lancelot's sword-bridge in the Arthurian legends. After that, Gurdjieff arrives at the remote monastery, which, like Shambala (the place of happiness in Tibetan Buddhism), is completely surrounded by mountains. That is similar to concepts of an inner holy of holies or sanctum. Such images are found in many writings: from the Swedish mystic Emanuel Swedenborg (1688–1772), the founder of Theosophy Helena Petrowna Blavatsky (1831–1891) and the writer and specialist in Buddhism Alexandra David-Neel, to the scholar and writer on religion Mircea Eliade, who only recently died. But the symbolism doesn't end there: the monastery also contains three main areas, which are obviously linked with the cosmic Law of Three.

At this mystic place, Gurdjieff receives the two important revelations which will later form the basis of his teachings: the Enneagram and the holy dances, which remind him of Sarkis Pogossin's physical exercises.

The monastery of the Sarmoun Brotherhood – whose name may make us think of Sarman, the divine essence in the Zoroastrian religion – seems to me to describe a place within the soul, rather than an actual geographical location.

Whether this is so or not, it is assumed in Gurdjieff groups that this brotherhood has been active for more than 4,000 years as a 'protector of tradition'. An important part of this tradition consists in knowledge about the use of the Enneagram as a universal, cosmic symbol capable of explaining all life processes.

It is also therefore assumed that the Enneagram appeared about 2000 BC in the Middle East, when the gods of Middle Egypt were encompassed in ninefold forms (Enneads). The use of the Enneagram was then preserved and protected for thousands of years as a secret lore, by a more or less unknown brotherhood, until the beginning of our century when Gurdjieff came upon this cosmic diagram and made it known to the West.

How could a knowledge which had been carefully preserved for millennia suddenly be revealed at the beginning of this century, far from its cultural source?

Who is the guiding force concealed behind the Sarmoun Brotherhood, which seems in some unexplained way to be connected to the Sufis?

These are unanswered questions. There are wild speculations that the legacy of the Sarmoun Brotherhood was passed down to the Naqshbandi Dervishes, and that we are in fact dealing here with early Christian impulses – but none of this is convincing. In this view of the Enneagram's history we encounter too many secrets, which I believe have been intentionally grafted onto it to mislead the naïve seeker.

Another interesting possible explanation was suggested to me by Arnold Graf Keyserling and the publisher Bruno Martin, who have both been very involved in the 'work'.

The starting point for their suppositions is that the word 'Sarmoun' can be translated as 'bees'. The Sarmoun Brotherhood corresponds with the bees, who obtain their nectar from many blossoms; the brotherhood, in other words, gathers its knowledge from many sources. It is likely that this refers to the Neo-Platonists of the 9th century AD, who were known as the 'pure brothers of Basra'. This was a brotherhood influenced by the Greek philosopher Plotinus (c205–270), who can be considered one of the forerunners of the Christian mystic tradition. But we should also remember that Gurdjieff did not think very highly of the Greek philosophers. He said they were like anglers, who 'invented various "sciences" because they were bored with the bad weather'.[1]

One of Plotinus' teachings says that the soul must purify itself through imaginative perception. And as we have already seen, the Enneagram provides an excellent help for clear and objective self-knowledge – and thus purification. In addition, the philosophy of the later Neo-Platonists has a surprisingly developed tendency towards systematic methodology, a love of complex, diagrammatic systems. This led the 'pure brothers of Basra' to propound nine states of existence, based upon a threefold division of the world into mineral, plant and animal realms, each grouping being divided again into three within itself.

In spite of many similarities, though, there is no direct reference to the Enneagram in the *Kitab Ihwan As-Safa*, the philosophical work of the 'pure brothers of Basra'.

There have also been persistent speculations that the Enneagram could have arisen from Pythagorean philosophy, in which the uneven numbers had particular significance. It was not only the Pythagoreans, though, but also all of Greek antiquity that had special respect for uneven numbers. But Neo-Platonists, including the 'pure brothers of Basra', were particularly drawn to Pythagorean ideas.

Bennett, for his part, assumes a Chaldean[2] origin of the

Enneagram, since it is built up on characteristics of the numbers three, seven and nine.

To be honest, the exact source of the Enneagram remains a secret. Since both Gurdjieff and Ichazo connect it with Sufi brotherhoods, it is probable that this universal cosmic symbol is related to the Sufism of the Middle East. But everything else is shrouded in the mists of history, and cannot be much more than speculation.

The Enneagram as mandala

I only became aware at an astonishingly late stage of my Enneagram studies of something that should have been perfectly obvious: that the Enneagram can be seen as a simple form of mandala.

The Sanskrit word *mandala* has the literal meaning of 'circle', and thus refers to the cycle of life and the laws of the cosmos, which Jung said was always represented by the feminine archetype of the circle.

A classic mandala consists of:

- a middle point, which in the Enneagram is the mid point of the radius
- a circle which encompasses the whole
- varying numbers of cardinal points; in the case of the Enneagram, nine such points
- axial symmetry

All these preconditions are fulfilled in the Enneagram. One could almost imagine that Gurdjieff had himself invented it during his travels in Tibet.

The Tibetans were the last culture, apart from the Hopis, to make daily ritual use of mandalas. Since the conquest of Tibet by the Chinese in 1959, this culture has largely been destroyed. The mandala as archetypal symbol of man and the universe, of self-knowledge and the evolution of consciousness, seems now

Figure 11 *Simple mandala forms*

to be enjoying a revival in the West. For the last ten years or so, it has met with ever increasing interest.

In Tibet the mandala was seen as an instrument for transforming demonic forces. The Enneagram can also be understood as such. I would call those energies demonic which try to lead us astray into false ways of living. Like the mandala, the Enneagram also mirrors various levels of consciousness. With its help one can become aware of one's present state of consciousness; but it also provides a map which shows how one can reach higher stages of consciousness and transpersonal vantage points.

So the Enneagram as a special kind of mandala is a tool for facilitating the process of self-development. Like all mandalas, the Enneagram is also able to give shape and form to perception of the nature of reality. We can therefore view the Enneagram and the mandala as models of existence that help us to see reality more clearly.

The Enneagram is different from the usual mandala form, though, because of its ninefold division. Most mandalas have larger numbers of focus points, whose sum is usually based on multiples of four (eight, twelve etc).

The number nine

In Turkish regions and in Islamic culture in general – from which Sufism derives[3] – the number nine has always had special significance. In ancient Turkish tradition, the world is divided into nine spheres; it was said that 'there is nothing beyond the nine'.[4] According to the cosmology of Islam, the universe is composed of nine spheres, whose outermost ninth sphere is beyond even the stars.

There is no doubt that the number nine was highly regarded by all those influenced by Sufism. It seems very probable to me that the Enneagram does derive from this tradition. Nine as the embodiment of fulfilment is also ultimately connected with the nine months of pregnancy leading to human birth. In antiquity, the nine was regarded as the number of perfection. In Islam there are 99 names and attributes of God, which in turn give rise to the Islamic prayer string of 99 beads.

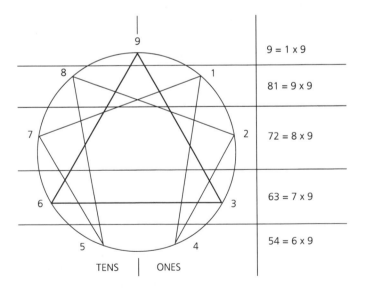

$9 = 1 \times 9$

$81 = 9 \times 9$

$72 = 8 \times 9$

$63 = 7 \times 9$

$54 = 6 \times 9$

TENS | ONES

Figure 12   *The nine in the Enneagram*

One could produce many examples of the way in which the nine is seen as the archetypal symbol of a completed cycle. In most languages, the root of the word for 'nine' is connected with the concept 'new'.[5] But now I would like to return once more to the Enneagram itself and demonstrate the various combinations of the nine which it contains.

As in classical Greek culture, playing around with the characteristics of numbers was very popular in the Arab world of the early Middle Ages. In those days people did not have such a quantitive relationship to numbers as we do; numbers were felt to be symbolic of qualitative aspects of the world.

Figure 12 shows that the Enneagram not only has nine points, but that the nine is also present in each pair of points. If we divide the Enneagram into five horizontal sections, the number sequence of each section produces a multiple of nine. The nine permeates the Enneagram on every level, which is due to the fact that our decimal system, derived from the Arabic, is based on the same laws as the Enneagram.

If we examine the lines of the hexagram in the Enneagram (1, 4, 2, 8, 5, 7), we can see that its product is again divisible by nine:

$$1 + 4 + 2 + 8 + 5 + 7 = 27 \quad 3 \times 9$$

The nine is therefore directly and indirectly present at all levels of the Enneagram. The completion of a full cycle is therefore also potentially contained at every level. From every single Enneagram point we can set out to achieve perfection and completion.

For those who may be interested in the mathematics of the Enneagram, I would like to add a further astonishing observation, again centred upon the nine. If we multiply the number values of the points of the right side of the diagram with each other, and of the left side – as shown in *Figure 13* – their sums are divisible by nine; and, likewise, the products of the multiplied numbers given in each of the three sections of the Enneagram formed by the equilateral triangle (points 3, 6

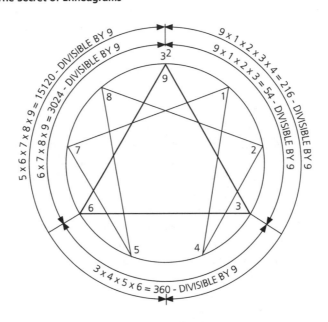

Figure 13   *The sum products of the Enneagram sections*

and 9) are also divisible by nine. The nine is like the spiritual essence imbuing the Enneagram on all levels.

It is highly likely that the Enneagram was developed when Arabic and Indian mathematicians introduced the number nine in Europe in the latter part of the 9th century, and revealed its significance. Nine completes a cycle, which can then begin again on a new level with the number ten.

I would like to mention in passing that nine also plays a special role in Buddhism: 108 qualities are attributed to the Buddha, which is why the Buddhist *mala* (or prayer string) contains 108 beads. The sum of 108 contains the nine (1 + 0 + 8 = 9). Nine is therefore also a symbol of perfection and cyclical culmination in the east Asian culture of Buddhism.

Notes

1 Gurdjieff, G I, *Beelzebub's Tales To His Grandson*, Vol. 3.

2 The Chaldeans came to power in Babylon in the 7th century BC, and possessed a mathematical system that was very developed for that time.

3 The Sufis were (usually mercilessly persecuted) mystics of Islam, who were active in the Middle East from the 9th century onwards.

4 Taken from: Endres, Franz Karl and Schimmel, Annemarie, *Das Mysterium der Zahl. Zahlensymbolik im Kulturvergleich.*

5 For example, in French 'neuf' also means 'new', and in German 'neun' – 'new' is 'neu' [transl.].

CHAPTER 3

==

The Geometrical Figures of the Enneagram

. . . everyone believes that the truth he perceives is the only one.
. . . All truth is simple.

Rodney Collin

An Enneagram consists of three elements: the circle, the equilateral triangle, also called the 'divine triangle', and the irregular hexagon (hexagram). If we draw a line through the top point of the triangle and the mid point of the circle, this straight line forms the axis of symmetry of the Enneagram. That means that the forms right and left of this line exactly mirror each other. As we will later see in more detail, the moment of transition from the right to the left side of the Enneagram – in other words from point 4 to point 5 – is particularly problematic. On the right side of the Enneagram we find the causes or preconditions of a process; on the left side we encounter the effects of these causes.

The equilateral triangle creates a division of the Enneagram into three equal parts, which reflect the three stages of the process of passing through the diagram. The hexagram is a very irregular and eccentric form, whose vertical axis of symmetry provides an important point of reference. The lines of the hexagram and triangle are not connected with each other; they overlay each other and have 15 points of intersection.

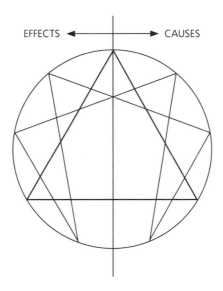

Figure 14 *The axis of symmetry of the Enneagram*

This arrangement of the three elements of the Enneagram (circle, triangle and hexagram), gives rise to a strangely 'regular yet irregular' form. The perfect spatial character of the circle is divided by the pronounced symmetry of the intersecting lines. This is reminiscent of Islamic geometrical forms, whose balanced symmetry occupies their internal space, and can thus represent the creative powers of Oneness (Allah).

The circle

The symbol of holistic thinking is the circle. The circle embodies and communicates an integrated totality of knowledge in many traditions, for example in Native American tradition (medicine wheel), Buddhism (mandala) and even in Christian culture (the halo).

The circle is the archetype not of a static but of a highly

dynamic wholeness, which arises through the confluence of two opposing and at the same time mutually complementing forces. Every circle always has two directions of movement: clockwise and anticlockwise. Just as the earth's orbit is determined by two opposite forces (rotation and centrifugal force), so the path of human beings and of all existence depends on the interplay of such forces: conscious and unconscious, awake and asleep, male and female, attraction and repulsion. The circle itself is actually composed of two such opposing aspects. It symbolizes the path through these opposite poles, and reminds us that such a path can never be a straight line. Emma and Carl Gustav Jung see the circle as a symbol of the path of individuation, of self-realization in other words, which can only be attained through confrontation with the paradoxes of life.

The nine Enneagram points are to be found on the circumference or periphery of the circle. The process described by the Enneagram proceeds clockwise through these points, from point 1 to point 9. So the circle represents our perception of a time-sequential process or event.

For clarification, let us return for a moment to the practical example on page 3 *Figure 6*): I recognize my unhappiness, realize what is causing it, become active in opposing it, and thus enter into those conflicts and tensions of which my suffering consists; then finally – if all goes well – I complete the process, having attained happiness and contentment. That is a time-sequential and also a logical process, which corresponds to our normal linear modes of thought. By following the course of the circle in a clockwise direction, I can recognize and analyse the logical sequence and the time sequence of a process. The path leading from Enneagram point 1 to point 9 encompasses my specific intention and aim.

In certain respects, though, this circle is a symbol of our head, and 'our head is round so that thinking can change its direction', as the avant-garde philosopher Francis Picabia tellingly remarked. Circular thinking (in contrast to linear) tries to see truth from many different standpoints, so as to understand the whole.

If we follow the Enneagram's circle in an anticlockwise direction, therefore, we can recognize quite clearly the circumstances that need to be borne in mind if a particular process is to meet with success. The observer stands at the goal, the end of the process, and looks back on the path which would have led her there. This is an ideal perspective, from which vantage point she tries to plan all the preconditions which will need to be fulfilled if she is actually to attain her aim. It is also a perspective which looks back to the present from the future. There is much wisdom contained in such a method; it is one particularly characteristic of English mythology, and has a connection with the magician Merlin.

The sequence of clockwise Enneagram points represents the functional cycle of a process; the anticlockwise direction offers a total overview of an ideal, completed process. While the latter reveals all the steps needed to attain the ideal, the former is an excellent means of keeping in mind all the precise details that need to be considered for a process to run smoothly. In our example of unhappiness, the observation of the sequence of individual necessary steps (in a clockwise direction) corresponds with the functional view of the person involved. If we observe this process from the perspective of its ideal attainment, and ask: 'How can we really become happy?' it is best to visualize this ideal as precisely as possible, so as to perceive its real qualities and characteristics.

The triangle

Gurdjieff and Ouspensky started from the premise that the human being possesses three centres through which life-energy is mediated. Enneagram points 3, 6 and 9, which form the equilateral triangle, divide the form into three equal sections, corresponding with these life-energy centres. We can characterize these three sections of the circle as described in the following sections.

First section

Enneagram points 1 and 2 are connected with our body and its automatic, unconscious reactions. According to Gurdjieff's view, the human being reacts in this phase like a machine operating on an action-reaction mechanism. It is this stage also which burdens us with neurotic, repetitive and compulsive behaviour. So in this section of the Enneagram we are dealing either with the material description of an outer situation, or with clarifying the basic conditions necessary to a certain process. Points 1 and 2 can be seen as the material preconditions that will subsequently allow a process or sequence to unfold.

Second section

At Enneagram points 4 and 5 we encounter actions which alter something in the interior world, in the realm of feelings. Our actions, whose foundations are the material preconditions marked out by Enneagram points 1 and 2, bring us closer to our desired aim. These two points of the second segment of the circle represent the changes which are necessary to continue a process in a way that is focused upon its ultimate goal.

Third section

Points 7 and 8 represent the attainment of our goal and 'work'. In the area of personal development, this third section of the Enneagram embodies the intellect, which organizes and directs our experiences (particularly those of the second Enneagram section) towards attaining our goal. This is the realm of mental and spiritual results of a process. Gurdjieff himself describes the aim of the 'work' to be that of freeing yourself from a compelling self-identification with your inherent passions and preoccupations; and also from being influenced by external factors.[1]

Gurdjieff characterizes the three 'shock points' of the Ennea-gram (points 3, 6 and 9 – which we have not yet dealt with, but will return to in detail later) as: 'Holy Affirmation' (point 3), which is localized in the brain, as function of the intelligence; 'Holy Negation' (point 6), which is an automatic form of reaction originating in the spinal cord; and 'Holy Reconciliation' (point 9), which is a heart-warmed power of feeling corresponding to the nerve junctions or synapses of the human body, and which is particularly concentrated and active in the solar plexus.[2] It is our task in life to try to unite and combine these three centres with one another. We all know the times when our heart and head tell us two different things. We know what it's like to be pulled in two conflicting directions at once. This is caused by an insufficient cooperation and connection between our emotional, intellectual and motor centres. At those painful moments when we are incapable of making decisions, they are working against each other.

A typical symptom of this inner conflict in our society is the intellectualization or rationalization of feelings. You may, for example, catch yourself thinking about whether you still love your partner – in which case your intellectual centre is dominating your emotional centre, which is sure to cause you emotional difficulties. When all contact between the three centres is broken off, death occurs. In *Beelzebub's Tales*,[3] Gurdjieff says that the death of many pyramid thieves and of the first archaeologists who opened the burial chambers, is connected with this principle. The ancient Egyptians, said Gurdjieff, concentrated the 'Holy Power of Atonement' in their burial chambers. When these chambers were opened, this power, combined with the forces at work within the people who entered there, caused such disharmony and disruption in them that they soon died. Exactly why the first archaeologists to enter the king's chamber of the Great Pyramid at Giza all died soon afterwards, is a riddle that science has still not yet solved. But it surely says something about the potentially deadly nature of such disharmony and conflict.

Gurdjieff always emphasized that his chief work, *Beelzebub's Tales*, can be read and understood on three different levels – head, heart and body (or instinct). These three levels correspond with an outer, an inner and a deeper meaning. One can only truly understand this book by activating all three centres in the reading of it. On the highest level, the three sections of the Enneagram correspond to genuine individuality, true will and objective consciousness. But the ultimate stage is far in advance of our consciousness – we can only have an inkling of it.

The three Enneagram sections are clearly differentiated by the speed of reactions, actions and insights that occur in each one. In the first, the *motor* or *automatic circle-segment*, the human being reacts very quickly. The movement centre represented by the first and second Enneagram points is the one that develops furthest through natural processes alone – is 'given' from birth onwards. The learning in this realm takes place largely through the principle of imitation. This movement centre has been most thoroughly investigated by the physicist and therapist Moshe Feldenkrais (1904–1984).

In the second, the *emotional circle-segment*, the human being reacts noticeably slower. It is in this realm that the most conflicts usually occur. Since our society is lacking in institutions for schooling and cultivating emotional sensibility, the emotional centre of most Middle Europeans is frighteningly underdeveloped. In a culture like ours, which is dominated by the male archetype, it is extremely hard to develop or express qualities inherent in the archetypal feminine.

In the third or *mind circle-segment* of the Enneagram, we react most slowly. This is the realm upon which our society concentrates all its efforts at education.

To illustrate the varying reaction speeds at work in the three realms of the Enneagram, let us imagine that we have just narrowly avoided having a car accident. The following sequence of events is typical.

- You are driving along a road with poor visibility, and suddenly a child runs out in front of you.
- First your movement centre reacts (section 1 of the Enneagram): quick as lightning you avoid the child or brake hard.
- Then your emotional centre takes over (Enneagram section

2): you may well experience uncontrolled – often hysterical – emotional reactions.

- Finally, once you have nearly got over the shock, your mind centre (Enneagram section 3) comes to terms with what has occurred by thinking about it, and by imagining what might have happened.

The three kinds of human nourishment

The way that eating is organized by Bennett at Sherborne House is also closely connected with The Enneagram. Eating and drinking were very important in Gurdjieff's view, and Bennett related the Enneagram to all that is necessary in preparing and eating a meal. First the kitchen itself must be prepared; then the ingredients are chosen; the meal is cooked,

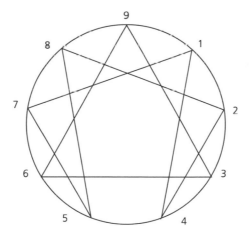

		9	Life
8	Eating the meal	1	The kitchen is ready for cooking
7	Serving the meal	2	The work in the kitchen begins
6	The community for whom the meal is being cooked	3	The ingredients
		4	Preparing the ingredients
5	Cooking		

Figure 15 *The kitchen as cosmos*

served, eaten; and finally everything must be cleared away again. In this process, the kitchen corresponds to our body, the food to our experiences or soul, and the cook to our will or spirit: thus the kitchen is experienced as a whole cosmos. In what follows, though, we will be more concerned with other, non-material forms of nourishment.

According to Gurdjieff, we need three forms of nourishment:

- The food we eat
- The air we breathe
- The sense-impressions which stimulate us

The *food* we eat belongs to the first section of the Enneagram. Its transformation (in the second section) is essential to life. It provides the material basis for our existence.

The *air* we breathe belongs to the second Enneagram section. Humanistic psychology in particular has focused on the close connection between breathing and feeling, in such therapies as Rebirthing. In moments of fear we hold our breath; when we are relaxed and secure on the other hand, our breathing is calm and regular. In this feeling-imbued second circle-segment, we encounter our values, our strivings and unproductive tensions. It is here that we meet the physical expressions of suffering, as well as our power of imagination, our wishes and fantasies. We struggle to harmonize all these with the reality we experience.

The third section of the Enneagram is formed by our *sense-impressions*, which stimulate our thinking and challenge our powers of reason. It is here that a synthesis is created of all that was prepared in the first two sections. We arrive at our goal by learning to activate and integrate our body, feelings and intellect, and to master them. Recalling the image of the coach and horses, it now becomes possible for the Lord/Lady and Master/Mistress to tell the coach driver where to go. The driver obeys and controls the horses, so that they proceed in the desired direction.

The power that can transform the three kinds of nourishment into a higher principle is contemplative self-observation; this

allows them to become a 'Help to God'. But according to Gurdjieff, 'intentional contemplation-readiness' is required, otherwise the nourishment is not transformed in such a way
as to let us make use of its 'holy cosmic ingredients'.[4] If, for
example, we react in an automatic, associative way to the sense-
impressions we receive, we remain stuck in a mechanical kind of
reflex, and our nourishment is not integrated and transmuted.
Only when we break with our habitual mechanisms and act
consciously is it possible to transform our nourishment and
make it available to higher spiritual centres. The feelings
accessed by our breathing can be consciously used to nourish
the higher emotional centre; likewise, the intellect stimulated
by sense-impressions can serve as nourishment for the higher
mind centre.

In his autobiographical work *Life is Real Only Then, When 'I
Am'*, Gurdjieff speaks at the very outset of two almost deadly
wounds he received, which he viewed as compelling strokes of
destiny in his life. The first affected his body primarily: he was
wounded by a stray bullet and then fell ill with scurvy, and subsequently dysentery and malaria. He recovered from all these
physical afflictions. Later he was wounded by a bullet once
more, and this time suffered a mental crisis. He started to have
severe doubts about himself and his work, and was tortured by
the thought that his goal was still so distant and unattainable.
Yet this crisis of self-confidence allowed Gurdjieff's aim to rise
up clearly before him:

> . . . to destroy people's susceptibility to being influenced, which all
> too easily allows them to fall prey to the influence of mass-
> hypnosis.[5]

What Gurdjieff is in fact describing, concealed under the cloak
of autobiography, is nothing other than a process passing
through the three circle-segments of the Enneagram.

Just as one can interpret Gurdjieff's two bullet wounds as
Enneagram shock points, so it is also no doubt possible for all
of us to find decisive, ground-breaking moments in our lives.

But we should not view such shock points as static. If the Enneagram is to be of real use in our life, we will need to have a playful, flexible, living relationship to it, rather than seeing it as a fixed structure.

In my work as therapist I have found that people can nearly always identify two shock points in their lives. The first almost always occurs in early childhood, as an outer event: the death of a beloved grandmother for instance, or decisive rejection by parents, in some form or other. It is quite natural that we react negatively to this first sort of shock: we want to defend ourselves at all costs against the pain and injury connected with it.

The second shock usually puts an end to the negativity which has wormed its way into our lives as a result of the first, childhood shock. In general, the second decisive point is actually a consequence of the first, but it now leads to a change of direction: it may be that such a change comes about through a therapist, a spiritual group or, more seldom, through a close relationship of love and trust with another person.

It is typical for the period following the first shock to be characterized by repetitive or even compulsive forms of behaviour. Fear of intimacy, addiction to outer recognition and praise, negative attitudes to life and feelings of inferiority, are often at the root of such neurotic patterns. The second shock brings more independence and inner as well as outer freedom. It is common at this point to separate from a partner, in spite of the fear that this causes; by doing so we can discover that happiness consists in self-reliance; and this in turn makes us available for a new quality of relationship.

I have found that it is very helpful to search for these two shock points in one's own life. By recalling the first shock, the sorrow and/or rage connected with it can be released. Expressing these feelings purges us, and opens us to new, deep experiences. We frequently become aware of the first shock only after the second has occurred; we need the relative security attained through the second shock in order to be able to cope with knowledge of the first. The three Enneagram sections also correspond with three different stages of consciousness to which Gurdjieff's method refers:

- Exoteric schooling, by means of which the outer personality is formed and knowledge is accumulated.
- Mesoteric schooling, through which the emotional centre is formed as the basis for a true ego around which the personality can coalesce.
- Esoteric schooling, in which the human being experiences a rebirth and begins to make use of her higher spiritual centres.

This threefold division of all processes underlies the observation that cause (action) and effect (reaction) cannot by themselves explain how processes unfold. These two aspects require a third, a uniting force that has a balancing and harmonizing influence upon the relation between cause and effect. We are often unaware of the actual nature of this force. We only feel and observe that it is has an active and altering influence. The force of mind or intellect, and of love or the higher self are similar to this, in that they often work in unseen ways, enabling us to attain our goal. *Figure 16* clarifies these connections.

By meditating on our solar plexus, we establish contact with the automatic and physical aspect of ourselves. If, on the other hand, we meditate upon our heart, we make contact with our feelings. And when we concentrate on the inside of our head, we clarify our intellect and the sense-impressions that stream into us. To unite all three sides of the Enneagram in a complete, dynamic form, we need to meditate upon our head, heart and solar plexus simultaneously. This is not such a difficult exercise, and allows us to balance perfectly the three sides of the inner Enneagram triangle.

This is the daily practice of those involved in the schools of the Fourth Way (of Gurdjieff, Ouspensky and Bennett). It can lead to full self-remembering, and is, at the same time, a good way of preparing the body for the conscious assimilation and transformation of its three forms of nourishment.

Figure 16 *The three stages of consciousness in the Enneagram*

Gurdjieff calls the cosmic law of threefoldness 'Trimazikamno', an invented word which embodies his idea of above and below combining to give rise to a mediating centre. This concept also refers to the physical process that occurs during self-remembering. The cosmic threefold law, in connection with the three forms of human nourishment, is by no means just a theoretical or metaphorical construct. People who practise self-remembering can sense the workings of this law in their own body. If a sense-impression (third form of nourishment) enters our consciousness at the precise moment that we remember ourselves, the fact that we then sense our heart gives us a physical experience of the threefold law; it provides a clear indication that our emotional centre is assimilating the sense-impression. We try not to lose ourselves in this sense-impression though, either through association or day-dreaming, but to remain aware of our physical feeling and of ourselves within the body. At the same time we experience how we are absorbing the sense-impression. This is usually accompanied by an inner motion – often experienced as a rush of energy, a kind of delicate stream of warmth, or as a light shower – which flows down from the heart to the navel region, to the solar plexus, then ascends again to the head: chest (heart), stomach and head – as the centres of feeling, movement and mind – are then all equally involved in the process of assimilating the sense-impression.

For the second form of nourishment, the air, representative of our contact with the world of emotions, we can observe the same sequence. The necessary precondition for a conscious relationship to air depends on trying to stop identifying with our negative emotions. Once we have managed to do this, we then enter into the process of remaining self-aware. The feeling

Figure 17   *The threefold division of the Enneagram*

impulse can, once more, be clearly sensed as a stream of warmth flowing from the heart to the abdomen, and then back to the head where it is consciously grasped.

More intellectually orientated people may, as they practise self-remembering, experience a stream flowing down from the head to the solar plexus, and from there up to the heart. The heart, as emotional centre, then provides the uniting force, which it is as capable of doing as is the head or mind-centre. The fact that the body can form the third, harmonizing element between opposites, is the basis for many esoteric 'movements'. Systems of self-development such as yoga and Tai-Chi also make use of the body as a mediator between emotions and intellect.

We can only really understand this cosmic Law of Three, as embodied in the Enneagram, once we can sense the three forces or centres in our own body.

The third force

The idea of three forces has a long tradition. We find it in the Vedas, the oldest texts of Indian literature, as well as in the teaching of the three gunas in the Vedanta. Originally the three gunas were described as the forces which determine all variety and differentiation within the world. Astonishingly, they correspond perfectly with the law of threefoldness that permeates the whole world of phenomena. The third, or divine force, has the task of helping the world towards a higher plane of existence.

The alchemists, who projected their own inner experience upon the world of matter – in their day still largely unexplored – also recognized the threefold law as an archetypal force at work in all life processes. The classical alchemistic oven had three openings, by means of which the transmutation process took place.

Mercurius – or quicksilver – was regarded as the harmonizing substance whose neutralizing influence mediated between the

Figure 18   *The alchemistic oven*

world of fire (sun, or consciousness) and the world of water
(moon, or feeling). This third, usually invisible force, gives
significance and meaning to a process. It mediates between Yin
and Yang, male and female, above and below. The polarities
between matter and soul, body and feeling etc, are overcome in
the third part of the Enneagram through the power of mind.
The uniting force of intellect gives rise to the new quality

towards which we have been striving. This is exactly what the alchemists wished to express in their concept of the dynamic Mercurius. The third force is what keeps a process flowing and moving. If a process comes to a halt, it is usually due to an insufficient third force.

In line with modern concepts of physics, let us assume the three fundamental forces at work in the universe to be space (passive), time (active) and a mediating dimension as third force (neutral). Static space in this concept symbolizes the potential energies of a situation. Dynamic time controls the transformation and application of these forces and potentials; and the neutral, mediating force harmonizes the interaction of the two other energies.

It is typical of Gurdjieff's teaching that he provides two different versions of the threefold law, which differ from each other in their descriptions of the third force. One version is formulated in terms of the higher (active) principle uniting itself with the lower (passive) principle, in order to give rise to the mediating centre.[6] By 'higher' is meant whatever is beyond the normal range of our perception. For the sake of simplicity we could call it the 'spiritual'. The 'lower' on the other hand means everything of a material, sense-perceptible nature. To show what this means in concrete terms, let me return to my example about writing this book on the Enneagram. My hand and the pen, or the keyboard of the computer, need to combine with each other to allow the writing to happen. My hand serves the spiritual or mind impulse and therefore corresponds to the higher principle, while the pen or keyboard are forms of matter. The mediating principle, which arises as a new quality through their conjunction, is the writing itself. Neither my hand alone nor the computer or pen can write by themselves. Writing therefore requires the uniting of higher and lower principles. According to Gurdjieff, we are largely unaware of this mediating quality, of the third force; in other words we fail to see that our writing (for instance) represents a new entity and quality that was not there before. So we do not perceive the threefold law.

In his second version, Gurdjieff sees the third force as a kind of catalyst that allows a reaction to occur between the two other forces. In terms of physics, this third force then corresponds to a field of energy, similar to the electromagnetic field of an atom which combines nucleus and electrons to form the fundamental atomic structure. In the example of writing this book, the idea of writing about the Enneagram creates a specific motivation (force field) which brings together the hand, as instrument of the higher principle, and the computer keyboard, as instrument of the lower, and allows them to work productively together.

The American astrologer Rodney Collin has drawn attention to the fact that the elements of threefoldness – movement (body, passive), feeling (soul, active) and intellect (spirit, neutral) can alter their positions within this model depending on their relative situation and perspective. This has already been illustrated in *Figures 8* and *9*, pp. 17 and 18, and reminds me of Albert Einstein's Theory of Relativity (1905). Gurdjieff's view, of course, is focused on whether our motor, emotional or intellectual aspects are more developed; whether, in other words, we derive our nourishment more from bread, air or sense-impressions. People in each of these three groups look at the world in a different way, and develop along different lines. If one relates this triad of forces to the 'work' of the schools of the Fourth Way, three steps are revealed:

- Self-remembering (Enneagram point 3)
- Division of awareness (Enneagram point 6)
- Consciousness (Enneagram point 9

Gurdjieff views consciousness as a state in which we know what we know, yet at the same time also see how little and contradictory that is. The highest stage of consciousness, symbolized by the ninth Enneagram point, comes into its own when the human being is wholly aware of her activity and simultaneously experiences herself as her own observer.

Playing around with the number three

To conclude this section on the threefold law, I would like to show that the Three, like the Nine, permeates the Enneagram on all levels.

Each of the three sections of the Enneagram contains a multiple of three. But if we look at the sums obtained between one triangle point and another, we will notice that the first, the physical/motor section is characterized by 5×3. Leonardo da Vinci demonstrated the symbolic connection of the Five with the human body, and drew the human being as a pentagram within a circle. The second, emotion-based section, contains 2 times 3×3. The Two corresponds with human emotion, which arises from the soul's duality between feelings such as love and hate, and the urge towards life or death. The third section, the mind or intellectual section, contains two times the 5×3 characteristic of the body, as well as five times the 2×3 which characterizes the emotions. It is also an astonishing fact that by

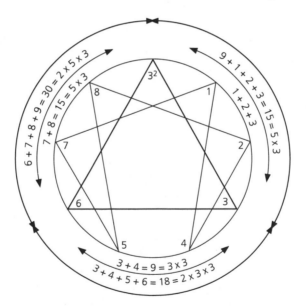

Figure 19 *The three in the Enneagram*

multiplying 5 × 3 × 2 (in other words, the various numerical elements of body and feeling), we obtain the product 30, the number characteristic of the mind or spirit.

This means that in the third section of the Enneagram the elements of the two other sections are contained and combined. So the experiences one gathers in the first two Enneagram sections are integrated and we become self-determining. Like the quicksilver of alchemy, we can now move freely, and can become a messenger of the gods.

The three shock points in the Enneagram

We have so far ascertained that the Enneagram divides every process into three different sections, organizing it in such a way that we can gain an overview. But to keep a process flowing and moving, outer impulses, stimuli or shocks are necessary.

To attain its aim, every process in the Enneagram requires

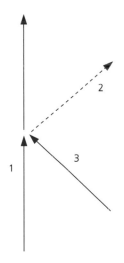

1   The first impulse.   The first movement
2   The tendency for the first movement to be sidetracked
3   The shock or outer impulse, which knocks the first movement back on course

Figure 20   *Shock and direction in the Enneagram*

outer impulses that should be neither too strong nor too weak, and that should occur at exactly the right moment. When a process has reached point 3 or 6 of the Enneagram, such moderate shocks not only maintain its dynamic, but also simultaneously focus and direct it towards attaining the goal. The shock points show us that no process in the world runs without some kind of interruption, just as no force continually flows in the same direction. Without these shock points, every occurrence would sooner or later come to a complete halt, or go astray in quite unpredictable directions.

Every event usually causes one or more reactions, which usually cannot be calculated exactly, and which can make a considerable difference to its course and effect.

Let us return once more to the example of unhappiness (page 3, *Figure 6*). I feel unhappy and would like to alter this state of affairs. If no new outer influence enters my life at *Enneagram point 3*, it is unlikely that I will be able to attain my aim. It may be a therapist, a teacher or a book, but whatever form it takes *something* external must come towards me for my life to take a new direction. To understand this principle we may have to stop thinking of ourselves as lonely heroes who determine their lives without outside help.

In the Enneagram, this point 3 is described as the 'mechanical shock' – as something external, in other words, that has an altering effect on our physical life. In my example of writing this book (page 20, *Figure 10*), the preparation of the material conditions is followed by applying the idea, or one could say the content. If we look at the human being's personality structure, the psyche appears at this first shock point as a new quality.

If no new quality arises and is assimilated at this mechanical shock point, the process exhausts itself instead in continual, mechanical repetitions. We then get bogged down in the misery of our own neurosis, whose irresistible power compels us to continue in its circular groove.

The second Enneagram shock point is to be found at the opposite point of the triangle, at *Enneagram point 6*. This shock is described as the 'conscious shock'.

Look again at the path that leads from unhappiness to happiness (page 3, *Figure 6*). Enneagram point 6 marks the point of my awakening. I am now in a position to use my own efforts to direct my life towards my chosen goal. It is not really until this second shock point that one can speak of an emancipated will that can direct itself in the way it intends. This is partly to do with the fact that at this second shock point we succeed in transforming negative feelings into positive ones by halting self-identification with them. I observe my feelings without allowing myself to be submerged in them. This corresponds with the 'evenly-suspended attention' that Freud so highly valued.

Another form of this helpful, impersonal approach, consists in viewing life in more playful terms than we usually do, as a game.

The second shock point is characterized by the number six; this is known as the perfect number, for it contains both the sum and the product of its constituent parts:

$$1 \mid 2 \mid 3 = 1 \times 2 \times 3 - 6$$

On the level of number symbolism, this means that the analysis (addition) and synthesis (multiplication) are combined with each other. At Enneagram point 6 we develop an overview; we see which separate, specific steps still need to be taken to reach our goal. If the need for changes and new directions at certain points is not recognized, functioning communities can suddenly fall apart, individuals can fall ill or even die and organizations can suddenly disband and go under.

Every radical change at the two shock points 3 and 6 of course brings considerable risks. One can never be absolutely sure in advance whether an outer impulse will appear, and how it will affect the existing system and process. The disintegration of nations like the USSR and Yugoslavia shows clearly that the effect of outer impulses can never be accurately predicted. It is also worth remembering that every goal-orientated process can be diverted from its aim by the reactions which it calls forth. At the two shock points 3 and 6, our process is synchronized with other processes of independent origin.[7] This means that it is brought into harmony with processes in the environment which are running parallel to it.

It seems that modern chaos theory confirms the Enneagram's premise of two shock points. A stable, ordered process does not tip over into chaos at some undefined moment. There are clear boundary points at which this can happen. These correspond exactly with the Enneagram shock points.

It also becomes particularly clear at these points that the Enneagram must always be seen in interaction with other Enneagrams. On the path I have described from unhappiness to happiness, the first shock point is connected with the Enneagram representing the therapist, teacher or author who has written the helpful book. The second shock point is also connected in the deepest sense with the Enneagram of a 'teacher'; this does not have to be an individual, but may appear in the form of a particular situation which affects one very deeply, or an essential and insight-provoking conversation with a partner.

For the sake of completeness, let me just mention the third shock point at *Enneagram point 9*. This is where we reach our goal, and are open to entering upon a new process.

The Enneagram shock points can be summed up as follows.

First shock point
Mechanical shock at Enneagram point 3
This is an outer impulse which gives new direction or impetus to a process. A new quality enters in, which directs the process towards its aim.

Second shock point
Conscious shock at Enneagram point 6
This transforms the available material and organizes it in accordance with the desired aim.

Third shock point
The aim, Enneagram point 9
The aim and goal of the 'work' has been achieved, and the system is ready to enter into a new process.

To make productive use of these shock point impulses, it is helpful when planning a process to follow the lines of the hexagram.

The hexagram

The hexagram is formed by the Enneagram points 1, 2, 4, 5, 7 and 8. The movement along its lines is reminiscent of a labyrinth: leading from above downwards, then up again, changing sides, down again, back up and changing sides once more; and then the whole sequence can start again from the beginning. In this backwards and forwards motion we find ourselves: like the cat with the hot porridge we circle our higher self and work our way towards its various aspects. Jung compared this movement gesture with circling the stupa in Tibetan Buddhism, and called it 'circambulation' (walking around something). Such movement is also characteristic of our life's path.

To get a feeling for this labyrinthine movement of the hexagram, it is a good idea to draw a large Enneagram on the ground and walk along its lines. One can best do this at the beach.

The fact that the hexagram is open at the base can be seen as symbolic of the process by which all creation proceeds from original wholeness and unity. In astrophysical terms, this unity is described as an undifferentiated gas cloud and the Big Bang.

As the original unity – which can also be seen as emptiness – differentiates itself, two parts first arise, which are portrayed by the right and left sides of the Enneagram. This first differentiation of creation also has a third aspect – the relationship between the two parts, which is as important as the parts themselves. Thus the primal movement of creation produces a threefoldness from emptiness. These three interrelating forces correspond to what we are familiar with in physics as proton, electron and the movement of the electron around the proton. These are active (A), passive (P) and neutral (N), otherwise they could not interreact with each other to create new atoms and molecules. In a certain sense, the six Enneagram points of the hexagram symbolize the six different combinations of these three fundamental forces (ANP, NPA, PAN, NAP, PNA, APN).

The open base of the hexagram offers us an image of how, from emptiness – the opening, which can also be seen as female genitals, womb or the alchemical vessel – six creative forces are formed. We know from modern fractal geometry[8] that such irregular forms as our hexagram represent the norm in nature – wholly symmetrical shapes are the exception.

This is the cosmological, and also physical, background to the hexagram in the Enneagram. We should remember that the cosmos and the human being abide by the same laws.

In fact, the hexagram is the most archetypal form of the Enneagram; Gurdjieff, Bennett and Rodney Collin make it quite clear that although every cosmos is an Enneagram, not every Enneagram has to contain a triangle.[9] Indeed, according

Figure 21 *Symbolic representation of the hexagram, after Eliphas Levi*

to Gurdjieff, the triangle within the Enneagram symbolizes the essence or, as he calls it, the 'soul' of a process. Unensouled processes do not need a triangle; in other words the hexagram is the central, vital part of the Enneagram. This accords with the views of the alchemists of the 17th century, who held that there are six cosmic processes, corresponding to the six alchemical operations.[10]

To see how we can work concretely with the Enneagram, we must turn our attention to the six Enneagram points formed by the hexagram. The hexagram sequence gives us the points 1, 4, 2, 8, 5 and 7. One can regard this as the will-cycle sequence (in contrast to the functional cycle given by the logical time sequence of a process). It is this sequence that is relevant to someone wanting to direct her will to attaining a certain goal, whether this lies within or outside of herself. To begin with, though, her observations remain on the right side of the Enneagram, while she turns her attention to her body (Enneagram points 1 and 2) and her emotional centre (Enneagram point 4). Afterwards, her perspective alters to the left side, as she concerns herself with her intellectual centre (points 7 and 8) and emotional centre (Enneagram point 5).

When investigating outer processes, the observer first analyses her material conditions (Enneagram points 1 and 2), which she relates to the product or the material to be transformed (Enneagram point 4). If she thereby arrives at a result, her aim will be clear to her (Enneagram point 8) and she will set to work accordingly to effect her material (product or service) so as to transform it (Enneagram point 5). The aspect of presentation, marketing and consumption and such like must also be considered, which occurs at Enneagram point 7.

The hexagram therefore illustrates:

- how, through will-power, we successfully change ourselves in regard to an ideal
- how we successfully plan and conduct a process or action
- how we analyse ourselves in a specific situation
- how we analyse a social or economic process

Perspectives in the Enneagram

My understanding of how to work practically with the Enneagram has been greatly helped by viewing the connecting lines of the hexagram and of the triangle as useful perspectives which open up when I stand at a particular point in the form.

Look once more at *Figure 6* (page 3), which depicts the path from unhappiness to happiness. To begin with I stand at *Enneagram point 1*. I feel unhappy. The helpful perspectives which open up to me lead my gaze towards Enneagram points 7 and 4. They offer a sight of my aim – to be happy once more – as well as of the defence mechanisms which I put in the way of my own happiness. In this perspective there is, therefore, a tension between the great effort needed to attain my goal and the possibility of failing to achieve it, of giving it up.

Following the hexagram lines, I confront my defence mechanisms. At this stage I am at *Enneagram point 4* and look towards Enneagram point 2. I therefore become aware of my repetitive patterns. But at the same time I have a view of Enneagram point 1, which revealed my unhappiness to me; keeping this important realization in view motivates me to persist in my actions and strivings.

From Enneagream point 4, still following the lines of the hexagram, I reach *Enneagram point 2*; at this point I can catch a clear sight of the form and substance of my aim (Enneagram point 8).

With well-formed ideas of what I am striving for, I stand at *Enneagram point 8*, and look towards *Enneagram point 5*, which begins to show me how I can make use of the energies contained in my tensions and conflicts.

Once I have come to terms with that, I gain a perspective of *Enneagram point 7*, which allows me to begin to serve my chosen aim. At the same time I know exactly what practical steps I still need to take to attain my goal.

If I observe the impulses which effect this process from without – which is usually impossible, since they are very difficult to predict – I move to Enneagram point 3 and look towards

Enneagram point 6. It also becomes apparent that the next time-sequential point, 4, only offers me a perspective on the right side of the Enneagram, that is on the causes (see *Figure 14*, p. 37), while at Enneagram point 5 I can develop a clear overview of the effects of my actions.

To use the individual connecting lines of the hexagram as sight-lines, is therefore very helpful if I wish to change or affect something in accordance with my aim. To be successful in my actions, I need to adopt the relevant perspective of the will-cycle on arriving at a particular point of the functional cycle. Such perspective corresponds to the inner course of a process. It is the direction in which an ideal, or objective (in the sense of 'neutral') observer would turn her gaze.

The possible perspectives in the Enneagram
The sequence in which an ideal observer would view a process (will-cycle)

1 towards 4: a view of the obstacles in a process, which become apparent after material conditions have been satisfied. The potential difficulties which appear once the details have been dealt with.
4 towards 2: from the standpoint of the obstacles and difficulties, a helpful view back to the preconditions of a process.
2 towards 8: a clear view of the aim.
8 towards 5: a helpful look back to see how the energies of a process can be used creatively.
5 towards 7: a view of the way to organize energies in order to attain the goal. At this point we receive the creative inspirations necessary for completing an action or process.

Other possible perspectives
1 towards 7: an initial, unrefined view of the eventual aim.
2 towards 4: a view from the stage of material preconditions towards the obstacles that may be expected in the process.
4 towards 1: a view from the stage of obstacles and difficulties

back towards the preconditions of a process. This perspective holds the danger of a vicious circle of automatic repetition.

5 towards 8: a clear view of the aim.

7 towards 1: this can often provide a view of a new, higher-level Enneagram process.

7 towards 5: a clarifying view back towards the struggle with creative, transformative energies.

8 towards 5: a perspective which almost always relates to a new Enneagram level (like 8 towards 2).

8 towards 2: a perspective which almost always relates to a new Enneagram level (like 8 towards 5).

The points

Having looked into the various geometrical figures contained in the Enneagram, we can now come to its separate points, and observe what qualitative content can be ascribed to each one. Understanding the potential inherent in each, will allow us systematically to draw up our own Enneagrams.

We will now observe the functional sequence of a process from Enneagram point 1 to point 8 (or 9).

At *Enneagram point 1*, the material preconditions are created which will allow us to make some use of our unhappiness or desire for action of some kind. We sense, at this point, the 'pioneer spirit'. We let ourselves in for the adventure, for the transformative journey. In the battle against our unhappiness, we become aware that life cannot continue like this.

At *Enneagram point 2*, we observe our material preconditions in more detail and possibly attempt to alter them here and there. At the same time we begin to understand our task and goal more clearly. By coming to terms with our preconditions, we realize something of the nature of the 'work' that we are taking on. At this stage we deal with the physical basis of the process; we come to terms with the body and its automatic motor reactions.

At *Enneagram point 3* (first shock point) a new quality enters

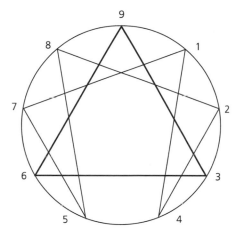

9   Transition to a new level

8 The aim is fully achieved	1 The material preconditions are provided
7 The first results are achieved; we begin to serve the task	2 Beginning to work with the preconditions, first activities, establishing contact with the task
6 Conscious shock point: a new, externally derived quality makes us conscious of the meaning of the task	3 Mechanical shock point: a new quality, task or aspect enters the system from without
5 Working at the task, suffering from the apparent unattainability of the goal, striving to direct and organize the task towards the goal – tensions	4 Striving to understand the task, penetrating deeper into the work; hindrances and difficulties appear that need to be overcome – tensions

Figure 22   *The separate points of the Enneagram*

in, without which the newly begun process would falter and fall asleep again. An external impulse provides a new quality, task or element, which gives us new strength, direction and determination to reach the goal.

At *Enneagram point 4*, we enter a new realm. Whereas Enneagram points 1 and 2 provided us with an understanding of the way in which our material basis was outwardly organized and arranged, Enneagram points 4 and 5 are concerned with the ways in which this material can be transformed. On the human level, this relates to feelings, for at point 3 the psyche appears on the scene as a new aspect and quality.

At *Enneagram point 4*, we have to struggle with obstacles and difficulties. There are things in us which seem insusceptible to change. In addition, our environment often tries to prevent us changing by its reactions. In a positive scenario, the obstacles are overcome at this point, and we can begin to penetrate the 'work' more thoroughly as we pursue our aims.

The transition to *Enneagram point 5* is the most difficult in the whole process. I will look at this in more depth in the next chapter. This transition is not a harmonious one: the contact with our point of departure is lost, without us having found a true connection to our aim. It is at this point, to take the example of writing this book once more, that I think I will never find the strength and endurance to give clear form and expression to all the different pieces of information about the Enneagram. I feel, it is true, that I must now write this book, since I have already worked so long at it, but at the same time it seems to me that I am incapable of doing so. I seem to have lost the 'thread' that was leading me from my intention to its fulfilment. Once this 'block'; in the example my 'writer's block', has been overcome – and it can last a long time – the goal begins to exert a strong magnetic power, drawing us towards itself and giving us confidence again.

At *Enneagram point 5*, I find myself involved in the 'work' once more, and suffer from the fact that although I have a clear view of the goal, it appears to be unattainable. I struggle to organize and direct everything towards the goal, and often become impatient – which gives rise to new tensions.

When no new external impulse enters the process at *Enneagram point 6* (second shock point), there is a danger that it will fizzle out. Such an impulse shows us with unmistakeable clarity what we need to do to attain our goal. If we are unhappy, we must wake up and stop going round in unproductive circles. In my example of writing the Enneagram book, the publisher appears on the scene at this point. The editor, or publisher's representative, helps bring the book to birth. Without this help, the book cannot be completed or delivered.

At points 4 and 5, then, we occupied ourselves with the material that required transformation; at point 6, a new, helpful impulse gave the process new life; at Enneagram points 7 and 8 we can now turn our attention to the goal and purpose of our work.

At *Enneagram point 7* the first results are forthcoming and are presented to the outer world, or are simply visible to it. We can now take some pleasure in these results and terminate the process, or continue the creative work. According to Gurdjieff, every complete whole is composed of seven elements. At Enneagram point 7, therefore, completion is at last attained; something has been achieved. We can now decide whether to go further or not. In terms of self-development, we may be so fascinated by our first successes that we allow ourselves to be limited by them and advance no further; or we may continue to develop and evolve, serving not ourselves but what we have attained.

At *Enneagram point 8*, the goal is fulfilled, so that at Enneagram point 9 the process can continue on a higher level. But this can only happen if, at Enneagram point 8, we give ourselves up to the result and completion of the process, and so rise above ourselves. In Zen Buddhism it is said: 'Climb to the pinnacle of the mountain, then carry on climbing!'

At *Enneagram point 9*, we experience the mediating third force, the uniting power of the process (which I described in the section on the triangle). This uniting, neutralizing energy can be called love, which elevates us to a new level of consciousness. Enneagram point 9 represents the end of an old process and the beginning of a new one. The circle closes and starts again.

The following table gives an overview of the nine Enneagram points.

Right side of the Enneagram: causes

The material preconditions of the body

1   The material preconditions are recognized and observed. We realize where we are. The necessity for change becomes clear.

2   The material conditions are analysed, or extended. We become better informed about our preconditions and starting point. We take the first step towards changing our situation, and thereby become aware of the effort and work that will be required.

3   *The new quality; the mechanical shock.* To prevent the process fizzling out before it has properly begun, an external impulse is necessary. This helps to direct the process towards its desired aim. At this point we are often unaware how things will continue. But we receive help from outside, to which we need to be open. A new quality of the 'work' is attained.

The material to be transformed.

4   The difficult effort of the 'work' begins, which requires goal-orientated actions of us. Obstacles and hindrances that cause tensions make their appearance. We strive to overcome these, to prevent the process stagnating.

Left side of the Enneagram: effects

Aim and purpose of the 'work'

5   All that has been attained up until now must be systematically and consistently directed towards the goal. We suffer at this point because we fear that we will never attain our aim, although we can now see it clearly before us. We can no longer extricate ourselves from the process, since we have become so involved with it. We are frustrated because things seem to be moving so slowly. We have to learn to make positive use of our tensions.

6   *The new quality: the conscious shock.* Help comes to us once more from without. We take up the new impulse and digest it. Now we really become aware of what it means to attain our goal.

7   The new quality has been taken up. Now we serve our goal. The spiritual result of the work is outwardly presented or simply becomes apparent.

8   The goal is attained.

9   *The new quality: a new process begins.* End of the old and beginning of the new process.

The 'Hero's Night Sea Voyage'

The transition from Enneagram point 4 to point 5 represents a grave difficulty. Even purely visually, a great cleft is apparent between these two points. Gurdjieff called the recognition of this cleft 'Harnelahut' in his writings. It is connected with painful experiences. At this point the seeker doubts whether she's on the right path, whether all the effort is worthwhile, or whether she is perhaps totally unfit for such work.

In Gurdjieff's second book, *Meetings With Remarkable Men* (in the chapter about the tragic death of Soloviev), I believe that Harnelahut is symbolized by the Gobi Desert. The truth-seekers do not know how they can cross it, yet do not give up their plan in spite of all their doubts. They do not dare to enter the desert on unknown paths since they cannot carry enough water with them and are threatened by sandstorms. This illustrates the need to find new paths and ways. One has to undertake a process with sufficient emotional tension and longing (symbolized by the water). In addition, the seekers must (in scarcely veiled symbolism) discover something that has been buried under the sand. Gurdjieff seems to me to be describing the state of transition between points 4 and 5 of the Enneagram, and to be saying that one needs a great power of emotion to sustain oneself through the despair that is experienced there. To get any further, one has to find new – that is individual – paths, so as to reveal things which are deeply buried within oneself.

We are at the transitional point between the right and the left side of the Enneagram. We experience the right side (points 1–4) as passive and unconscious suffering. We feel unhappy, discontent, and long for something without either knowing what it is or how we can attain it. The left side of the Enneagram is also formed by suffering, but now we accept it consciously. Conscious suffering feels totally different.

My personal experience of this was to realize that happiness is not the purpose of my life, however hard I may strive for it. I had to give up this illusory dream. And at that point, astonishingly, I felt happier than ever before. At the transition from the right to the left side of the Enneagram we are forced to jettison many (pleasant) illusions. But in so doing we come closer to real liberation.

Think of the challenge of mountain climbing: it is common to start feeling that we will never reach the peak. But when we look back, we find that the valley also lies unreachably far below us. We have to pass through this tension between 'I will' and 'I can't'. This is what Jung meant by the 'Hero's Night Sea Voyage': a condition in which we are confronted by the soul's shadow-side, in doubt and feelings of inferiority. If we want to accomplish the leap from Enneagram point 4 to point 5, we *have* to take conscious suffering upon ourselves. When Jung asked a Tibetan lama why people of today are so distant from God, he replied that it was because modern Western man does not suffer deeply enough. In this respect, the whole of Western humanity has collectively reacted in ways similar to the seventh Enneagram type as described by Ichazo and the Jesuits (see page 117). But we need this process of suffering, whose function it is to destroy our illusions – which is very painful of course.

We need to experience darkness and distress if we are to attain personal perfection. Gurdjieff groups always stress that you cannot laugh all the way to your goal, that struggle is part of the path. In such groups, in fact, self-development sounds fairly terrifying: inner bankruptcy is a prerequisite of attaining a self-chosen, spiritual aim. It is only from the tension of personal collapse that we find the energy, through pure desperation, for further development. This collapse causes such stress that our programmatic way of behaving is interrupted – we can no longer react in an automatic, mechanical fashion. It is only when we have in some respect gone off the rails, that a new path can open up for us.

This process also informs the Christian gnostic tradition. In Enneagram terms, the right side of the form corresponds to the 'broad' path paved with material considerations and desires. The left side, in contrast, is characterized as the narrow path, that involves work and service, yet leads to liberation. Whether this should be seen as stale, killjoy moralizing, or as empirical perception and knowledge, I am not in a position to judge. I have, as you might suspect, the greatest difficulties with this kind of dualism; and as the Enneagram predicts, it arouses all my opposition. In my group not long ago, I asked very disgruntledly whether I was just here to suffer; and my teacher replied firmly: 'Yes!' When I protested, he told me the following anecdote about Gurdjieff: after a very large Shashlik meal, Gurdjieff was asked how he felt. He replied: 'I am happy that I feel so ill. I feel discomfort at 19 separate places in my body. I would be unaware of these places otherwise, so I am thankful for this successful outcome.'

Gurdjieff has a very similar attitude towards suffering to that found in Freud's theory of sublimation. In spite of all their differences, both considered it necessary to consciously refrain from desire-fulfillment in order to develop and make cultural progress.

The heptagon

If you look carefully at the Enneagram you will see that the intersection points of the equilateral triangle and the hexagram form an irregular heptagon inside the Enneagram. This inner heptagon plays an important role.

When, in 15th-century Europe, the significance of the zero was discovered, the periodic numbers were also found: that is, repetitions of particular number sequences which appear at regular intervals. They arise when, for instance, the number one is divided by three or seven. Divided by seven we get: 0.142857142857142 . . . The sequence 142857 reappears an infinite number of times and is identical with that of the Enneagram hexagram.

The periodic sequence 142857 symbolizes the course of a process that is constantly making a transition from one dimension to another. This algebraical expression of the periodic number makes the Enneagram a three-dimensional figure and shows that the individual Enneagram points should really be imagined as a spiral rather than a circle.

This periodic sequence (1–7) also demonstrates how every process needs to renew itself in order to continue. In modern physics and biology, people speak of the 'dynamic self-

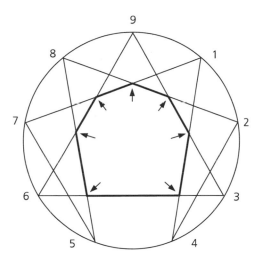

Figure 23   *The heptagon in the Enneagram*

regulation of the universe', and this refers precisely to this sequence, which is given pictorial form by the Enneagram's hexagram.

The fact that this form and its intersection with the triangle gives rise to an irregular yet perfectly symmetrical heptagon, again demonstrates the importance of the number 7 in the Enneagram. Every phenomenon possesses seven aspects, which, according to Gurdjieff, also contain two gaps or irregularities, giving rise to the law of ninefoldness underlying the Enneagram.

William Shakespeare (1514–1616) refers, in Jacques' famous speech in *As You Like It*, to the 'seven ages of man'. Rudolf Steiner speaks of the seven-year cycles in human life; and the religious historian Boris Mouravieff[11] believes that the law of seven rules all movements in the cosmos. The number seven appears, then, to be closely connected with human evolution and development; and the heptagon, likewise, seems to be the dynamic core of the Enneagram.

In esoteric tradition, the seventh ray of creation is seen as the one which expresses the structuring of Creation. And the Enneagram is really nothing other than a dynamic model by means of which creations, large and small, can be structured and analysed.

The Enneagram and the chakras

The inner heptagon of the Enneagram can be related to the seven chakras, the energy centres of the human body. This allows us to order the chakras as seven different levels of consciousness.

All chakras are an equal distance from each other, except for the solar plexus chakra (Manipura) and the heart chakra (Anahata), which are further apart both from one another and from the other chakras.

The base chakra (Muladhara) and the sex chakra (Svadhishthana) are both connected to the physical, material side of the Enneagram (points 1 and 2).

The throat chakra (Vishuddha) and the Third Eye (Ajna Chakra) belong to the spiritual side of the Enneagram, points 7 and 8.

The crown chakra (Sahasrara) that leads into other levels of consciousness, belongs logically with Enneagram point 9.

Up to this point, the correlation is clear and obvious. The heart and solar plexus chakra, however, do not easily fit easily with any specific point.

The gravitational centre of the body, the hara or solar plexus chakra, lies between Enneagram points 3 and 4. It is at this stage that positive struggle comes into play. Earthed and anchored by our physical preconditions, we fight against the obstacles and hindrances which appear at Enneagram point 4.

The heart chakra, described by the Sufis as embodying the 'intelligence of the heart', becomes active between Enneagram points 5 and 6. Without this we cannot reach the second shock point. Just as the solar plexus chakra represents the gravitational centre, the heart chakra symbolizes the middle (or fourth) point of the body's seven energy centres.

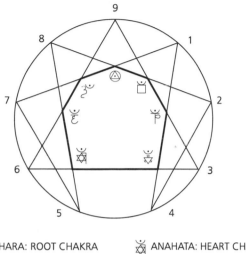

□ MULADHARA: ROOT CHAKRA

☿ SVADHISHTHANA: SEX CHAKRA

☿ MANIPURA: SOLAR PLEXUS CHAKRA

☿ ANAHATA: HEART CHAKRA

☿ VISHUDDHA: THROAT CHAKRA

☿ AJNA: THIRD EYE

△ SAHASRARA: CROWN CHAKRA

Figure 24   *The chakras in the Enneagram*

To come back to the solar plexus chakra for a moment: an important Gurdjieff exercise is to experience struggling quite alone, and winning through. If you decide to battle with another person, or better still an institution, in full consciousness, and not to give up until you come out on top, you will quickly discover your moral limitations; and also very likely find within yourself completely new and unexpected forms of behaviour. This exercise will also provoke questions in you about the purpose and sense of combat. Just try it! But be sure to observe your behaviour as precisely and consciously as possible. To imagine doing this is quite different from actually doing it. By carrying out this exercise you will become very aware of the way in which your solar plexus chakra works.

The chakras and the Enneagam

1	*Base chakra* *Enneagram point 1*	Everything begins at the lower end of the spinal column, where the life-energy (kundalini[12]) sleeps and wishes to be awoken.
2	*Sex chakra* *Enneagram point 2*	We proceed from our creative preconditions towards a goal or another person. A contact arises which allows us to gain better access to ourselves.
3	*Solar plexus chakra* *Enneagram points 3 and 4*	Important here is the struggle against hindrances through 'work'.
4	*Heart chakra* *Enneagram points 5 and 6*	The 'intelligence of the heart' opens us to a new quality.
5	*Throat chakra* *Enneagram point 7*	At this point occurs the intellectual representation of our experiences – both in the form of interpersonal comparison of experiences and as analysis of processes.
6	*Third Eye* *Enneagram point 8*	The goal, the spirit, is attained.
7	*Crown chakra* *Enneagram point 9*	We can now proceed towards new levels.

So it becomes clear that the path of consciousness development through seven archetypal stages, the chakras, corresponds to a large extent in both content and structure to the nine archetypal levels of the Enneagram points. At five places there is even an exact correlation.

The figure on page 75 and the table on page 76 illustrate the relation of the seven chakras to the separate Enneagram points. The two 'physical centres' (heart and solar plexus chakras) are to be found between two Enneagram points, and form the focal gravity point of this cosmic diagram. It is not only in Enneagram terms that these lower points represent the greatest point of difficulty. One of the most arduous transitions in the energy-centre system is that between the solar plexus chakra – coming to terms with one's own aggression and will-power – and the heart chakra – the heart's power of feeling.

Notes

1 Gurdjieff, G I, *Beelzebub's Tales*, Vol. 3.

2 Gurdjieff, G I, *Beelzebub's Tales*, Vol. 1.

3 Gurdjieff, G I, *Beelzebub's Tales*, Vol. 2.

4 Gurdjieff, G I, *Beelzebub's Tales*, Vol. 2.

5 Gurdjieff, G I, *Life is Real Only Then, When 'I Am'*.

6 Gurdjieff, G I, *Beelzebub's Tales*, Vol 2. Also interesting in this connection is Salzmann, Michel de: 'Footnote to the Gurdjieff Literature' in *Parabola*, New York, August 1980, Vol. 3, page 751.

7 For more detail on this see: Bennett, J G, *Transformation oder die Kunst sich zu wandeln;* and Bennett, J G, *Hazard – The Risks of Realization*.

8 Fractal geometry demonstrates that specific regular chance models correspond to the irregular forms at work in nature. It investigates these models. One central discovery of fractal geometry consists in the fact that in nature – for example, in coastlines, trees and mountains – symmetrical forms almost never appear. The contemporary mathematician Benoit Mandelbrot is regarded as one of the pioneers of this non-Euclidean geometry.

9 Collin, Rodney, *The Theory of Celestial Influence*. On pages 90 and 222 there are some Enneagrams without triangles.

10 These are: *coagulatio* (fusing), *dissolutio* (dissolving), *sublimatio* (refining), *putrefactio* (fermenting), *separatio* (separating) and *transmutatio* (transformation). These six processes are produced by the various reactions of salt, sulphur and quicksilver (mercury).

11 Mouravieff, Boris: *Gnosis*, Book 1. *Studies and Commentaries on the Esoteric Tradition of Eastern Orthodoxy*, page 95.

12 We must remember, though, that in contrast to Indian Yoga philosophy, Gurdjieff did not believe that waking the kundalini was necessarily beneficial for human development. Gurdjieff considered kundalini as nothing other than the primal organ 'kundabuffer', whose effects had been misunderstood by Indian philosophy. He also mistrusted Yoga philosophy, in which kundalini plays an important role, since he thought this system did not develop all three centres of the human being in a simultaneous and harmonious fashion. However, I see kundalini as symbolic of life-energy: it is just a question of how one deals with it and implements it.

CHAPTER 4

The Psychological Types

> It is the greatest mistake to believe that the human being always
> remains a constant unity. He never stays the same for more than
> a short period. He continually changes; he rarely stays the same
> even for a single hour.
>
> *G I Gurdjieff*

In recent times the Enneagram has become known as a model
of nine psychological personality types. This idea, put forward
by the Chilean psychologist Oscar Ichazo, contrasts with
the teachings of Gurdjieff and Ouspensky, who both view the
undeveloped or sleeping human being as a collection of many
different egos. The pioneers of the Arica School have really only
adopted the outer form of the Enneagram, without entering
into its inner dynamic, as described by Gurdjieff. But it is not
my intention to disparage the Arica School and its successors.
They have made the Enneagram into a useful psycho-diagnostic
model, whose strength is its ease of application. The basis of
this psychological Enneagram system is that there are just nine
– no more and no less – fundamentally different personality
types. The Jesuits, in particular the influential American Jesuit
priest Bob Ochs, emphasized the fact that the Enneagram
can make us aware of our shadow-sides without any need for
moralizing.

The Jesuits started from the premise that the nine types of
the Enneagram represent nine independent types of defence

mechanism, which they regard as sin. They are sinful because each specific type does not live out his wholeness (which lies in the total reaction-potential of all the types together), but is ego-centred. In spite of all the differences between the two points of view, one can find a clear parallel here with Gurdjieff's opinion that human fallibility and error is caused by egotistic tendencies. We do not attain wholeness because we cultivate our ego instead of exercising the duty of 'Partkdolg' – developing oneself through conscious suffering. Like Gurdjieff, the Jesuits assume that living fully through the ego means separating oneself from the world and from wholeness. This separation gives rise to a distorted view of reality and therefore also a false self-evaluation. In Gurdjieff's terms, the ego prevents us from remembering ourselves.

An important objection to this typology, I believe, is the view of Gurdjieff and Ouspensky that separate types never actually get as far as forming; according to the situation, external impulse or mood, different egos get the upper hand in us, determining for a while our feelings, thoughts and actions. Soon we come under the influence of other impulses, and a different ego then gains control over the personality. In other words, there is no ego-unity to be sensed within us.

Everyone can observe the dynamic of the different egos within themselves: when the sun shines and all seems rosy, when someone loves us perhaps, then our good sides, or the positive egos, come to the fore. But if the weather changes to an oppressive, cold grey, if we don't know how we're going to pay our taxes, or if something goes wrong, then our mood also immediately changes and the negative egos take control. Just observe your moods in connection with external events and you will be amazed to see how many different egos dwell within you, making you appear generous, fussy, open, withdrawn, friendly or aggressive according to the particular momentary situation. So where is your individuality in all this? If we are not highly developed people, our life expresses itself through a whole collection of many different types. Gurdjieff writes about the 'normal' person:

His ego changes as fast as his thoughts, feelings and moods, and he is subject to a huge error if he believes he is always constantly the same. In reality he continually becomes a different person from the one he was just a moment before.[1]

Somewhat later, Gurdjieff amplifies this:

The characteristic mark of a modern person is the absence of unity in him . . . [2]

Only those 'awoken' people, who have internalized the teachings of Enneagram point 6, can be called individuals – and it is only to an individual that a psychological typology can be applied. The 'automatic' person – and these are the large majority – passes, either more quickly or slowly, through all of these types in succession. He may first be the 'Striver', (see 'The nine personality types', page 90) then the 'Beginner' or 'Planner'. If all goes well he may seem to be the 'Optimist' (Enneagram point 7), but if things take a bad turn, he withdraws and becomes the suffering 'Observer' (Enneagram point 5). Everyone can watch this process going on in themselves. I am also rather bothered by the rigidity of Enneagram typology. The nine types invite one to assess oneself and identify with a particular category. But this can make us fall asleep instead of awakening us. These nine types remind me of what Wilhelm Reich (a follower of Freud) called 'character', or still more drastically, 'character armour'.[3] To behave more or less constantly as one of the nine Enneagram types is the same as building up a defence system against other forms of experience. This defence mechanism usually arises as a result of fear of identifying too strongly with our environment. Fear of losing our identity, or our consciousness of style and image, lead us to identify with one of the nine types on offer, without considering what other potential forms of reaction and behaviour we are excluding. Ultimately, the nine Enneagram types represent a neurotic defence system – one that no doubt helped us when we were children to survive the threat of withdrawal of affection and love, but which has, in the course of our subsequent socialization, grown solid and inflexible. The nine Enneagram types can thus be seen as nine different strategies for obtaining love. But unfortunately, such rigid, one-sided forms of behaviour put love beyond our grasp, for love is a child of freedom and fluidity!

In spite of all contradictions and contrasts, I would like to try at this point to relate the Enneagrams of Gurdjieff and of Ichazo to each other. Both systems have helpful aspects, and I have a practical suggestion for bringing them closer together – without, however, trying to disguise their deep divergence.

In what follows I intend not only to explore the nine Enneagram types, but also to offer my own typology. This is not for the purpose of advocating identification with them, but to describe nine different possible forms of reaction or expression that are available to every person.

When the first books about the nine Enneagram types came out, I was curious to see which type fitted me. There were types that I would happily have identified myself with, like the 'Artist' (Enneagram point 4 in Eli Jaxon-Bear's version[4]) or the 'Magical Child' (Enneagram point 7 in Jaxon-Bear). There were types I rejected, like the 'Smart Three-in-one' (Enneagram point 3 according to the theologians Rohr and Ebert[5]) and the 'Reformer' (Enneagram point one according to Richard Riso[6]). At last – thank God! – I managed to categorize myself: yet I still looked over my shoulder with envy at other types, thinking that I also possessed certain qualities of the 'Artist' and 'Magical Child'. With the shock of self-knowledge I suddenly realized that aspects of myself were also quite in tune with the 'Smart Three-in-one' who likes to compete with others and pull out all the stops to beat them, as well as with the moralistic 'Reformer' who lifts his phallic forefinger in a fatherly gesture of admonition. I was, at last, freed from the burden of having to be just *one* of these types!

It is worth remembering that the Enneagram teaching comes from the tradition of the Fourth Way. It was the aim of this school to break down the automatic habits of its pupils, so as to free them and waken them in preparation for 'higher tasks'.

The Enneagram typology can help us recognize our own fixations and rigidity. The strength and weakness of the psychological approach to the Enneagram lies in its view of pathology. If we spontaneously recognize ourselves in one of the types, there is a good chance that we are in the process of becoming fixed in its structures and patterns of reaction – even more so if we feel at home in the role associated with it. We should also always keep our eyes open for which type we reject. Those we find unbearable, frightening or dreadful correspond to our shadow.

The shadow is the side of us that we reject and so are forced to project on to others. When I read about Enneagram point 9 in Jaxon-Bear's book and think: 'That's a perfect description of my awful neighbour: her hypocritical pretence of friendliness, her greed, her misguided efforts to be accepted – just dreadful!' then I can be sure that this hypocritical snake actually dwells in me. It would be more fruitful to find out how these behaviour patterns manifest in me than to hate my neighbour.

So it is important to pay particular attention to types who do not seem to fit us at all, and to whom we also respond negatively. We will often have a strong emotional reaction to these types, or think that the description of them is contradictory, and that such people don't exist. Rejection of the shadow can assume many different guises. According to Jung, working with our shadow is the precondition for self-knowledge.

To sum up: all nine types of the Enneagram dwell within us and can be seen, in Gurdjieff's terms, as the various egos which at different times gain control over us, usually in a quite tyrannical fashion. This view leads us to six action-strategies (in my system no separate strategies are allocated to the three shock points), which correspond with the behaviour repertoire, as it were, of our 'Chief Ego'.

The six strategies for human action

We all have the potential for implementing the six different action-strategies. This does not of course mean that we always make full use of this possible range of choices. We usually have our particular preferences and dislikes which prevent us from exercising any extensive freedom of rational choice.

Some people have a predilection for intellectual reaction, and for observing the surrounding world scientifically. Such people will tend towards the strategies embodied by Enneagram points 7 and 8. An emotional person, on the other hand, will automatically gravitate towards the strategies of points 4 and 5, feeling the intellectual approach of points 7 and 8 to be alien. Whoever is usually spurred to action by his motor centre will tend towards the first two strategies (Enneagram points 1 and 2), and will very likely reject both the intellectual and emotional strategies.

The following Enneagram of the six strategies for human thinking and action can help us recognize the one-sided nature of our view of the world and so begin to free up our rigid ways of acting and reacting.

At *Enneagram point 1*, it is important for us to have an outwardly perfect situation. That gives us security: so we make great efforts to sort out our material level of existence. We can, it is true, have an experience of our shadow here (Enneagram point 4); and since it upsets our harmony we project it immediately onto the 'nasty neighbour', the 'stupid boss' or anyone else. This one-sided strategy finds a path to more fluidity if we dare to line up Enneagram point 7 in our sights, so that we start to observe ourselves more consciously, or even serve the community in which we live. It helps if we can stop being too uptight, and start looking a little beyond our own garden fence.

The action-strategy at *Enneagram point 2* is characterized by activity. We try to assure our happiness by constant, diligent activity. This uninterrupted activity is often driven by fear of our own feelings. But we can't escape them; what we need, instead, is to pause and look towards Enneagram point 4, which confronts us with our own moodiness and daily frustrations. The view towards Enneagram point 8 shows us the possibility of a more mature and reasonable strategy, that can liberate us from

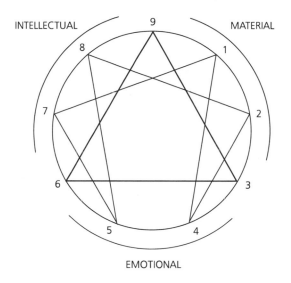

INTELLECTUAL   9   MATERIAL

EMOTIONAL

9 Body

8 As a strong person I demonstrate reason and cleverness in my actions. *Learning objective*: dedication to the task.
7 As a communicative, extrovert person I am successful. *Learning objective*: serving the community.
6 Mind
5 I suffer from my dependency on my feelings and moods. I attempt to rule my emotions with my intellect and knowledge. *Learning objective*: emerge from self-imposed isolation.

1 If everything is made outwardly perfect, then I receive attention and am successful. *Learning objective*: Being relaxed, easy-going.
2 Through being dynamic and active, love and success are assured. *Learning objective*: listen to feelings, pause for thought.
3 Psyche
4 I drown in my feelings, and project things without control onto people in my environment. I view myself as a special but also misunderstood person. *Learning objective*: coming to terms with one's own shadow and living in the present.

Figure 25 *The six strategies for human thinking and action*

our one-sided workaholism – such as is represented by the typically American saying: 'Without action, no satisfaction'.

The two strategies at Enneagram points 1 and 2, are focused mainly on the organization and alteration of our outer, material situation; they teach us to observe our actual situation in a realistic and down-to-earth way. But they neglect the inner aspect, and our mental and spiritual capacities.

At *Enneagram points 4 and 5*, in contrast, we stand mainly before our inner world. Through this one-sided approach to life we are constantly dependent on our moods and emotions, which frequently rob us of the energy to address the external world.

This Enneagram model of action-strategies can be seen in terms of Hegel's dialectics: the thesis is represented by the forms of action of the first triad, the antithesis by the feelings which often impede action, and the synthesis is achieved in this process by means of the spirit or intellect, which, all being well, consciously informs the other two patterns of behaviour.

At *Enneagram point 4*, we observe the world from the point of view of our emotions, and often feel rejected and misunderstood by our fellows. It is helpful in such circumstances to train our sights on the action-strategies of Enneagram points 1 and 2, which relate to our outer, material situation. At this stage we can learn that both inner and outer worlds have their own reality and validity.

On the psychological level, this leads us to a recognition of our shadow, which we erroneously project onto the outer world although it is a creative aspect of our inner life. In terms of depth-psychology, we ask ourselves at Enneagram point 4 where our boundaries are, and where the outer world begins. Anwering this question is often made more difficult by our tendency to swing to and fro between living in the past and fear of the future. But if we can learn to live in the here and now, we are automatically saved from drowning in a world of feelings.

At *Enneagram point 5*, we still struggle with our feelings and react emotionally to our environment; but we also begin to use our intellects to exert an influence on these emotions. We have, at least, a perspective on the intellectual action-strategies (Enneagram points 7 and 8) although we have not yet achieved much distance from, or equanimity towards, our suffering and mood swings. At Enneagram point 5 it is quite likely that we are withdrawn or live in an isolated situation, and are therefore at the mercy of our moods. In addition, we are also likely to be very ambitious – wanting to be more developed than we think we are. Most vital here is to establish some form of communication with the outside world (Enneagram point 7), which alone can free us from isolation.

The *Enneagram points 7 and 8* are informed by an intellectual view of the world, which constantly strives to sustain its contact with both the emotional and material world. The Enneagram clearly shows us, as long as we keep its prescribed perspectives in mind, that we run little danger of being sidetracked into one-sided and rigidified attitudes. Enneagram points 7 and 8 are connected to both the material and emotional worlds, just as Enneagram points 1 and 2 connect with intellectual and emotional perspectives. Only points 4 and 5 stand on their own, isolated from contact with the other qualities of action and thinking.

At *Enneagram point 7* our action-strategy consists of communication. We try, through our power of communication – to which our society usually responds favourably – to assure ourselves of love and success. We are well liked because we are entertaining and witty. The danger at point 7 is to become too outward and superficial, which is why we should never lose sight of Enneagram point 5. Just as becoming more extrovert at point 7 can lead one out of the isolation of point 5, so the retreat and withdrawal of point 5 can be helpful and healing to the point 7 position. At a higher level of human endeavour, one should, at point 7, offer one's gifts and capacities in the service of a larger community, thus overcoming one's own egotism.

At *Enneagram point 8* we come to believe – just as in the Age of Enlightenment – in the power of reason. This stands in contrast to a romantic reliance on the power of feelings. But the two approaches can, luckily, be combined – which leads to us developing a responsible capacity for action, well earthed by its connection with Enneagram point 2.

These six basic action-strategies are all severely limited on their own; only in real connection to the other Enneagram points do they extend beyond their confines. In combination with each other they enlarge and augment the scope for flexible response to all sorts of different situations that come towards us.

It is also possible to see these six strategies in three sub-group pairs: the first group (Enneagram points 1 and 2) focuses mainly on facts and actualities; the second (Enneagram points 4 and 5) on the influence of inner pictures and imagination; and the third (Enneagram points 7 and 8) on expression through language and communication. This would give us the following model of Enneagram-based action-strategy.

Facts: material basis

Enneagram point 1   Recognition and perfecting of outer conditions

Enneagram point 2   Enjoyment assured through action

Imaginative pictures: emotional basis

Enneagram point 4   View of the world informed by emotions, in which striving is emphasized

Enneagram point 5   Withdrawal into oneself, in which suffering is emphasized

Expression through symbol and language: intellectual basis

Enneagram point 7   Communication

Enneagram point 8   Reason and thoughtfulness

Directions of movement in the Enneagram

Before we examine the way in which the nine personality types of the Enneagram can be ordered, we need to look at the direction of movement in the hexagram and the equilateral triangle.

The arrows in *Figure 26* show the 'therapy and healing direction'. The opposite direction to this is what I call the 'action direction'. If one proceeds on the inner lines of the Enneagram, in the therapy direction, from any Enneagram point to the

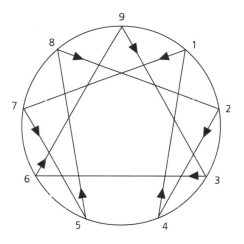

Figure 26   *The movement direction in the Enneagram*

next, one has the possibility of resolving neurotic patterns of behaviour. Enneagram point 1 is healed by moving towards the qualities of Enneagram point 7. Enneagram point 7 is resolved in the direction of point 5, which is in turn healed by moving towards point 8 etc. A person who is unsure and uncertain of himself, behaves as a typical representative of his Enneagram point. If he is stressed, he is likely to react in ways characteristic of the following Enneagram type in the therapy direction; if he is self-assured and relaxed, he is reacting in ways typical of the previous Enneagram type in the therapy direction. This is a psychological model which everyone automatically follows.

Let us look once more at the path leading from unhappiness to happiness (page 3). At Enneagram point 2 I become aware of my neurotic, repetitive patterns, which I can resolve by confronting my defence mechanisms against change of all kinds (Enneagram point 4).

The path through the Enneagram points from 1 through 7, 5, 8, 2 and 4, unburdens and heals me. If I follow the opposite direction, from Enneagram point 1 through 4, 2, 8, 5 and 7, then I act out my neuroses, in which case I burden myself more since acting them out reinforces them. If, in our example of 'working' at unhappiness, I become aware of my repetitive patterns (Enneagram point 2), my one-sided forms of behaviour are reinforced if I try simply to leap from here straight over to happiness at point 8. Such happiness will only be superficial, and beneath the surface unhappiness continues to grow, blossom and thrive. The extrovert patterns of Enneagram point 7 are intensified in the external focus of Enneagram point 1.

Relating this principle to the 'Divine Triangle', we can ascertain that the Enneagram teaching takes as its starting point the fact that the world of feeling (Enneagram point 3) finds its resolution in the spirit (Enneagram point 6), and the spirit or intellect its resolution in the body (Enneagram point 9). If, on the other hand, the life of feeling (point 3) acts itself out in a physical direction (point 9), this gives rise to an increased tension and conflict; and likewise, the body becomes full of tensions if the intellect tries to rule it.

The movement directions and the chakras

It is very revealing to relate the movement directions of the Enneagram to the inner heptagon of the chakras (see *Figure 27*).

We see here that the physical human being whose motor centre is connected with the lower spinal column (Enneagram point 1) finds balance in language and communication (Enneagram point 7) by guiding his energies up to the throat chakra. This is no doubt why people meet up in the pub after playing sport – after all, if they only wanted a drink, they could do that alone at home. A person who gives himself over to erotic sexuality (Enneagram point 2), finds resolution by concentrating on his focal point of gravity (Enneagram point 4) and confronting his own aggressiveness (also Enneagram point 4). The person who gets embroiled in fight and conflict (Enneagram point 4) does not find resolution by concentrating on his sexuality (Enneagram point 2), but is in far more need of physical

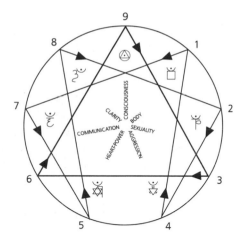

Figure 27   *The movement directions and the chakras*

movement (Enneagram point 1), which harmonizes and balances him. The 'heart type' (Enneagram point 5) finds resolution in the clarity of the Third Eye; and the intellectual (Enneagram point 7) heals himself by focusing on his heart power (Enneagram point 5).

These are, one can say, the 'seven inner types of the Enneagram' which give to the 'nine outer types' their particular quality and colouring, without being wholly subsumed by them.

In now turning our attention to the nine Enneagram types, it is important to remember how and where each type finds peace, healing and resolution; and how, also, the one-sidedness of each is reinforced.

The nine personality types

A fundamental belief of astrology is that a fully evolved individual unites within himself all 12 signs of the zodiac. Similarly, it is my premise that a fully evolved person combines all nine psychological types of the Enneagram in his behaviour repertoire. A flexible and conscious human being shelters within himself the nine different egos in harmonious balance with one another.

In the following observations about the nine types, you will very probably find one or two that relate particularly to you. These types will then represent your strongest or most tyrannical ego. It is also very important to discover which other type belongs to your therapy direction. It is advisable to involve yourself deeply with this other ego and to try, over a period of two or three days, to adopt its attitude and approach to life.

It is also very likely that you will find one or two types that you strongly disparage. If you were to meet such a person in daily life you wouldn't be able to bear him. You should also get to know this type more intimately, for it has the characteristics of your shadow.

In addition, it is very helpful to take a closer look at the type which lies in the 'action direction' of your spontaneously chosen type. You will find in it a type and attitude which you tend towards, but which is not helpful to your personal development. Its qualities will be ones which reinforce the one-sided ways in which you presently act. I will come back to these points as we look in detail at the nine personality types.

My view of these nine types is that their modes and patterns are definitely of positive use to us. Knowledge and awareness of all nine forms of reaction and behaviour will eventually lead to more freedom in our lives.

My characterization of the nine types is different – sometimes considerably so – from that of Oscar Ichazo and his school. This is because I have arranged the logical sequence of types according to the Enneagram points as they are viewed in the school of the Fourth Way.

My schema is as follows:

- Types 1 and 2 have qualities that are primarily focused on the physical

- Type 3 lies in the transition from the physical to the emotions
- Types 4 and 5 are primarily emotion-based
- Type 6 lies in the transition from the emotions to the intellectual
- Types 7 and 8 are primarily intellectual
- Type 9 lies in the transition from the intellect to the physical (new cycle)

Type 1: The 'Entrepreneur'

Looking at *Figure 28*, we see the 'Entrepreneur' – we could also call him the 'Beginner' – standing at Enneagram point 1. He belongs to the beginning of the Enneagram because he is very

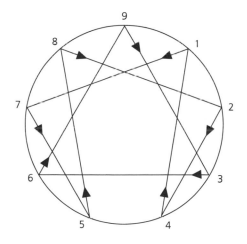

9	The Loving One (– passivity)		
8	The Mediator (+ resolving conflict – envy)	1	The Entrepreneur (+ economy – miserliness)
7	The Optimist (+ investigating – ambition)	2	The Planner (+ form – vanity)
6	The Hero (– power)	3	The Magician (– greed)
5	The Observer (+ healing – jealousy)	4	The Emotional Person (+ struggle – rage)

Figure 28 *The nine personality types in the Enneagram*

attached to the material structure of his life. The strength of the number 1 type is that he lives in the reality of the physical, material world, not in his imagination. He feels happy and self-assured when he has arranged his property and possessions to his satisfaction. This type corresponds to the root chakra (Muladhara) in the inner heptagon of the Enneagram, which is intimately related to the material basis of life.

The 'Entrepreneur' is not only gifted at budgeting and saving but he also actually enjoys keeping a close eye on his business and accounts, and investing his money. He reminds me of Uncle Dagobert from Walt Disney's Mickey Mouse films. Like Uncle Dagobert, the number 1 type likes wallowing in his money. The Franciscan, Richard Rohr, who considers himself a number 1 type, writes:

> What a wonderful feeling to save money! . . . I feel so much better when I can save. My conscience, formed in infancy, tells me it is better and holier to save money than to spend it.[7]

This dedicated preoccupation with the material basis of life is, however, fraught with a certain fear of poverty. Even if the 1 type is perfectly well off, the slightest financial hiccup will make him think he is going to land in the gutter. He is horrified to think that he may end up sleeping under a bridge somewhere. He doesn't see anything in the least romantic about this possibility. To avoid this danger at all costs he must have a nice tidy sum in his bank, or at least a regular income. The fear of coming a cropper often drives the number 1 type to pursue absolute perfection in his work.

Although material goods are usually the prime focus, this may not always necessarily be so. At Enneagram point 1, knowledge or friends can also be 'collected', which are then jealously guarded to make sure no one 'takes them away'. In terms used by Erich Fromm, this is a preoccupation with 'having' rather than 'being'.[8] Ultimately one can characterize this type by saying that he (unconsciously) tries to make up for the being-vacuum in his life by amassing possessions.

All of us have something of this tendency in post-modern society; but for this type it becomes the absolute focus, sometimes even an ideal taken to extremes of perfectionism.

The Enneagram type 1 is not invariably an independent entrepreneurial businessman or woman, but his capacities undoubtedly lie in the conscientious organization of finances and in self-reliance. One often encounters this type in middle management, which is where his gifts are best sustained.

If you are invited to the home of a number 1 type, everything will seem so perfect, well-ordered and clean that you may be afraid to breathe. You would be able to eat off the floor and the whole place may seem, in extreme cases, more like a museum than a place in which human beings live. If the physical environment is not ordered just as this type thinks it should be, he will feel threatened by dire chaos. He is also punctual and punctilious, hard-working and pedantic.

The 'Entrepreneur' is extremely communicative and happy as long as his financial situation is rosy. But if he encounters economic difficulties he will often react very badly, becoming aggressive, inflexible, and hard – one can practically see him freezing up in such situations. His latent tendency to miserliness breaks through, and one can observe him growing unbalanced and unpleasant. No one can please one of these number 1 types when they start grumbling and moaning.

The 'Entrepreneur' is thus very easily stressed by his material circumstances and his need to be successful. To reduce this stress it is very important for him to keep physically fit.

The archetypal figure we can relate this type to, is, it seems to me, the god Hermes or Mercury – the god of salesmen, thieves, travellers and athletes. Hermes or Mercury, with his winged sandals and wings, personifies speed. It is precisely here, in the physical-motor realm of the Enneagram, we find the greatest speed of reaction: the ideal 'Entrepreneur' type can decide things with lightning speed and react with complete assurance; he has his 'finger on the pulse' as the phrase goes.

The 'Entrepreneur' needs either physical movement or the flow of wares and goods. He is fascinated by activity and dynamics, and when he rests he rusts – or becomes, rather, a frustrated groucher.

Hermes/Mercury is also the god of all beginnings. In Homer he appears as a youth whose beard is just beginning to sprout. This type relates very much to the beginning of our life's path. According to Jung he is the guide who accompanies us on our psychological journey to find ourselves. All such journeys start with material preconditions, without which they cannot be undertaken.

When things go badly for the 'Entrepreneur', his shadow-side appears, as we have said. His susceptibility to stress makes him easy prey to psychosomatic illnesses, particularly since he finds it hard to express his aggression openly.

He has a tendency to be rather wooden and awkward in his love affairs. Love, with all its unpredictable emotions and upsets, doesn't suit him very well. He is often a passive recipient when it comes to choice of partner; if someone falls in love with him, he may not even notice it for a long time. To make it clear to either a male or female 'Entrepreneur' that you love him/her, you'll need to send an enormous Valentine card covered in red hearts and a large bunch of red roses! Once you get through to him though, you can educate him to be an exciting, entertaining lover.

It is healing for him to look towards Enneagram point 7 – the 'Optimist', whose strength is openness and communication. The number 1 type often shows interest in working in the media, which connects him with the seventh Enneagram type. A person who combines the two types in himself enjoys working in journalism, television or radio: the hectic activity prevalent in such professions suits him down to the ground, and allows him to thrive. And since the 'pure' type is a fairly rare phenomenon as we are usually determined by two egos in equal proportions, the Enneagram 1/7 mixed type is quite common.

Things don't look so cheerful when the 'Entrepreneur' combines with the 'Emotional Person' (Enneagram type 4), which he tends to do in stress situations. He then becomes too emotional, reacting too suddenly and nervously to all sorts of external influences, which he takes very personally. He becomes completely 'stressed out', and loses any overview, behaving like a headless chicken – which in turn makes him rage and rampage. In such a situation he feels completely at a loss, and is usually also haunted by his fears of impending poverty.

But if the 'Entrepreneur' combines with the 'Planner' (Enneagram type 2), this can lead to great material success since both types are on home ground in the material world. The mixture of these two, though, in contrast to the 1/7 type, often appears cold and impersonal and has a tendency to be a workaholic. When the number 1 type combines with the number 9 type, the

The 'Entrepreneur' or 'Beginner'

Strengths	Good eye for business; speed; good at making decisions; perfectionist
Weaknesses	Fear of poverty that can lead to meanness and rigidity; one-sided focus on 'having' rather than 'being'; unable to express aggression openly
Archetype	Hermes/Mercury
Resolved	Through Enneagram type 7, the 'Optimist'; communication has a healing influence
Hindered	By Enneagram type 4, the 'Emotional Person'; too many emotions make him neurotic and intensify his shadow-side (fear of poverty, rigidity etc)
Mixed types	1/7: healing; relatively common 1/4: intensifying neurosis 1/2: intensifying neurosis 1/9: is overidden by the influence of this archetype
According to Ichazo	The Idealist and Puritan with repressed aggression

qualities of the latter will override the former, since type 9, in its archetypal form, exercises a particularly strong influence.

The mixed types

In contrast to current thought on the subject, I am assuming that every Enneagram type can combine with every other. I, for example, am a number 7 type with pronounced type 3 tendencies. However, it seems to me that combinations mainly occur along the inner connecting lines of the Enneagram; and in addition, combinations with the previous and following signs are common. Of the eight possible combinations, four are relatively frequent and the other four less likely. I will only deal here with the four commonest 'mixtures'; anyone who likes can work out the others for himself.

If one of the types in a combination is an archetype (Enneagram points 3, 6 or 9), then the force of the latter invariably overrides the 'normal' type. The three archetypes, which represent certain primal forces, do not combine with one another: in other words, there is no 3/6, 9/6 or 9/3 combination.

Type 2: The 'Planner'

Like the 'Entrepreneur', the 'Planner' is an active person, who happily gets down to the business of daily life. He is often charmingly naïve, throwing himself into his tasks before he knows what's involved, and learning on the job. He is often ambitious and vain: he takes pride in completing his work in an elegant and attractive way. He would like to redeem the world through beauty. By taking such pains he hopes to win the recognition and love of those around him, for he is dependent on the opinion others have of him. The Enneagram type 2 manipulates his environment through beauty and action.

The 'Planner' corresponds to the sex chakra (Svadhishthana), under whose influence he would like to 'shine', and which endows him with radiant beauty. The aesthetic sense of the number 2 type feeds on this beauty. In his work he will often pursue a vision which combines beauty with the ideal of a better world. But he must also take care that his ideals and imaginations don't lead him into cloud-cuckoo-land.

It is vital for the 'Planner' to have a work and living environment that accords with his aesthetic need. If this is unavailable, he finds it difficult to work creatively. He feels best when there is something that can be formed in an ideal way, and when plans for the future need to be made.

The inner stimulus for his actions is a certain inferiority complex, so that his constant preoccupation is to achieve enough recognition to flatter his vanity. It would be dreadful for him to be overlooked and upstaged. As a child he had to win recognition by achieving things. He therefore suffers from a feeling of receiving too little love and attention, of not being loved for his own sake. But if these number 2 types get enough attention and interest from others, they can be astonishingly helpful and creative people, whose vanity and attention-seeking is hardly noticeable.

The archetype representing the 'Planner' is the goddess Aphrodite/Venus. She is a perfect mistress of the power of transformation, just as the 'Planner' has a constant need to alter what is there. He always wants to make things better and more beautiful than they are. His ideals remind me of those of the 'Bauhaus': functional, simple and beautiful. It is better to give him the praise and recognition he seeks than to withhold it, for otherwise he may well tyrannize his whole environment by trying to turn it into his stage and platform.

Aphrodite or Venus is honoured as the goddess of love and beauty, and as the archetype of the creative person. The 'Planner' goes through life in this mode: he seeks seduction and would love to seduce. He gathers around himself not only beautiful objects but also attractive men and women. In such a circle, the 'Planner' can become a visionary of genius.

If he falls in love, his partner can feel very flattered: he is certainly a beautiful person. As George Bernard Shaw (1856–1950) described in his play *Pygmaelion*, the 'Planner' does not hesitate to turn his partner into an 'exhibition piece'.

On the other hand, he also needs constant attention in a love affair. If he receives it, he will demonstrate his dream-lover qualities: love, though, is a dangerous trap for him, for he would happily deny himself just in order to be accepted. Many 'groupies' are number 2 types, for such types are sexually attracted by people who wield power. By accommodating himself to the other person, he loses himself, and his love and attractive, wild randiness can turn suddenly into hate.

I know a typical, attractive type 2 woman, who demonstrates a breath-taking desire to be submissive. She frequents high-class sado-masochistic clubs, dressed in skin-tight black leather, and enjoys being sexually used. Most type 2s do not live out this side of their sexuality, although their fantasies are often ruled by such thoughts.

Let me just mention at this point that Gurdjieff always said sexuality was one of the highest powers for positive self-development. He was doubtful, though, whether modern people were capable of dealing consciously with it. For this reason he recommended that we should live out our sexuality without connecting it to feelings.

Many of my readers, particularly women, will find that this suggestion smacks of chauvinism. We live in a state of conflict between two extremes: on the one hand we would in some ways prefer to separate sex and love; on the other, we long for highly unrealistic, romantic relationships. Neither the radical separation of feeling and sexuality, nor the the romantic concept of two people uniting in an inward harmony of love and sex, seem to lead to any lasting contentment. According to Gurdjieff, this is because people nowadays search for partners who simply don't suit them. Gurdjieff would probably recommend people of the post-modern age to observe their sexuality carefully in order to free themselves from mechanical compulsions; and to treat the state of 'falling in love' in a similar way.

Number 2 types often demonstrate a tendency to form symbiotic relationships once they feel they have found the right partner. But such a tendency quickly leads to problems in knowing any boundaries between oneself and the other. At least one of two partners wearing stylish matching outfits is likely to be a number 2 type.

It is revealing that Aphrodite/Venus was never forced into the role of victim. All her love affairs were mutual and she never suffered from rejection. This suggests a certain superficiality. The 'Planner' waves the banner: 'Deep people are neurotic' as he goes through life. It is precisely this lightweight quality that makes him so seductive! In psychological terms he demonstrates the slippery ease of the hysterical character.

The 'Planner' only gets 'deep' when he looks towards the

The 'Planner' or 'Shaper'

Strengths	Forming the future; has a sense for what is beautiful and practical, and a clear view of the future
Weaknesses	Inferiority feelings, which compel him to be proud and ambitious (lacking in emotional depth)
Archetype	Aphrodite/Venus
Resolved	Through Enneagram type 4; emotional depth has a healing effect
Hindered	By Enneagram type 8, the 'Mediator': the aspect of intellect and mind which this latter represents easily allows him to become calculating; his tendencies to pride and jealousy are intensified
Mixed types	2/4: healing; often achieved with increasing age (after middle age) 2/7: intensifies neurosis – often during youth 2/1: healing, like 1/2 2/3: rare, usually intensifies neurosis
According to Ichazo	The helpful woman (mother)

Enneagram type 4 perspective, the 'Emotional Person'. The latter is a type whom the 'Planner' often rejects out of hand. The type 4 person lives in a wholly contrasting way to the 'Planner'; but the weight of his suffering offers a healing balance to the light superficiality of the type 2, who is wholly focused on the future fulfilment of his desires.

In a combination of the type 2 with the type 4, we find a person who can manage to form himself into a 'beautiful soul'.

In stress situations, the 'Planner' tends towards the Enneagram type 8, expressing still more clearly than usual his negative characteristics of pride, vanity and ambition. He then becomes very calculating, losing his charming and attractive naïvety.

We have already looked at the connection between Enneagram types 1 and 2 in the section on the 'Entrepreneur' and ascertained that this is a positive combination.

When the 'Planner' falls under the influence of the 'Magician' (Enneagram point 3), he turns into the rather ambivalent figure of a wizard – like a youth with ruddy cheeks and shining eyes who, not wholly devoid of ambition and greed, would like to improve the world.

About the archetypes

At the three corner points of the Divine Triangle, at Enneagram points 3, 6 and 9, I believe that the primal forces or archetypes are at work. Not archetypes in the precise sense of the word, though. Jung described the archetype as an abstract, formative power which allows us to perceive images, but which is by no means the image itself. However, I am using the word in the way it is commonly understood, to describe the images and structures which derive directly from such formative, original forces.

The 'Magician' (Enneagram type 3), the 'Hero' (Enneagram type 6) and the 'Loving One' (Enneagram type 9) are all fundamental types who are not further divisible into other subcategories, and who are comparable to the gods of antiquity. The

'Entrepreneur' (type 1), the 'Planner (type 2), the 'Emotional Person' (type 4), the 'Observer' (type 5), the 'Optimist' (type 7) and the 'Mediator' (type 8) are, in contrast, derived or compound types. The first two types of the Enneagram are basically sub-types of the 'Magician' (type 3); types 4 and 5 coalesce to form the archetype of the 'Hero' (type 6); and types 7 and 8 reflect different aspects of the archetype of the 'Loving One' (type 9).

The 'Magician'

At the first shock point of the Enneagram stands the 'Magician', that archetype which demonstrates a mastery and ease in handling and manipulating things. But we would do the 'Magician' a grave injustice if we were to seek him only in the world of outer objects. He has a finely developed capacity for working with images and ideas – both his own and those of other people. He has a convincing gift for appearing self-assured, but his apparent search for outer prestige is ultimately the search for his true self. He strives to shed light upon the darkness of his own inner nature, and by succeeding in this he becomes an individual. Because he trusts in the enormous power of his psyche, miracles occur as he goes through life. Jung would speak here of synchronicity, while most people would look on him as always 'falling on his feet'. But the fact that he is also very industrious and ready to put time and energy into reaching his goal can often be overlooked. However, all this is only one side of the 'Magician' – and the one he would like us to see. He loves being thought successful above all else, and often fools himself and others without noticing it.

Ultimately one can say that the 'Magician' only involves himself with the external world in order to seek out the hidden driving forces of the psyche which underlie outer laws. To the other Enneagram types he may appear a person of status or prestige, but that is only a mask (to which, however, he is very attached) which assures him of society's acceptance so that, undisturbed, he can go about the business of following his inner ideas and pictures. The 'Magician' is as close to the imaginative worlds of dream and wishes as he is to the material world. His tendency to lie is not an evil propensity but dictated by his fantasy and imagination. Whoever invests so much in his outer image that he runs around like a walking trademark, has to identify himself with it at all costs. Since he is very keen to be thought of as 'someone' and to achieve things, he seems, on first sight, to be closely related to the 'Planner' and 'Entrepreneur'. But this aura of success is only one side of him; he is actually equally connected to the suffering, 'Emotional' type (type 4) and the 'Observer' (type 5). But he keeps his emotions closer to his chest. He prefers to appear distant and impersonal, so that he can first sound out situations and exercise power. When things go badly for him he has a marked tendency to depression.

The Enneagram type 3 has access to both the physical (first Enneagram section) and emotional (second section) levels.

The 'Magician'

Strengths	His connection to both the material and emotional world; his mastery of outer things through his power of imagination
Weaknesses	His craving for material success, power and status; his tendency to deceive and his lack of objectivity about himself
Resolved	Through Enneagram point 6, the 'Hero', from whom he can learn the attitude of service
Hindered	By Enneagram point 9, the 'Loving One, which strengthens his tendency to use his powers of seduction to achieve power and fame
According to Ichazo	The attractive person of status who often deceives himself

His position in the geometry of the Enneagram marks him out as the focal point between body and emotion. The number 3 type exerts power over both the material realm and the inner, imaginative world; but this can easily tempt him to want everything immediately, and to use his will and mastery (also of deception) to attain only material success and personal power. Such a type 3 person will spend so much time telling himself he is the greatest that he ends up believing it. He can thus get tangled up in a web of lies and deceit, losing all perspective on truth.

The type 3 always goes along with current sexual fashions: in bed, particularly, his animal symbol the chameleon comes into its own. He can offer whatever is wanted – Tantra, Tao-yoga, or just naïve kisses and cuddles – and adjusts to his partner with astonishing speed. In the sexual realm, the 'Magician' is capable of bewitching his partner beyond all bounds. He is the sexual partner everyone would like. His problem, though, is that he believes he is loved only for his sexual performance. In fact he lays more importance on professional recognition than on love.

Type 4: The 'Emotional Person'

Whereas the archetype of the 'Magician' forms a point of transition between the material world and the psyche, the Enneagram type 4 has both feet planted firmly in the world of emotions. What first strikes one about him is that he reacts to his environment and evaluates it in a highly emotional and sensitive way. In extreme cases he may drown in his feelings and be tossed hither and thither by them.

In psychopathological terms, the type 4 corresponds to the psychotic. His imaginative inner world is more important to him than the real, hard world of work. His subjective emotional state easily becomes his whole reality. This type can be liberated by overcoming self-obsession. The main conflict he is caught in is that of wanting to let go of his ego but being unable to do so. He soon learns that hanging on tight to his ego is what causes him suffering. It is therefore particularly healing for him to develop a religious conviction that connects him with something bigger than himself. Through self-remembering and regular meditation he can learn to use his reason to control his feelings and moods. This Enneagram type is continually faced by the need to develop the discipline of cleansing his mind from the shadows of his moods.

The type 4 struggles intensely between the light and dark in his heart; is frequently also plagued by (self-)doubt, which sometimes gives way to enormous feelings of happiness. To this type can be attributed the colour green (see next chapter) which combines the colour representative of light (yellow) with that of darkness (blue).

Because of his position between light and dark, the 4 type possesses a pronounced capacity for sexual feeling, with which he can easily seduce women and men of the other types, and even make them very dependent upon him. Yet this happens quite unconsciously, for the 'Emotional Person' dreams less of wild seduction than of romantic love. Tristan and Isolde – especially in Wagner's version – are his ideal lovers; his romantic world is imbued with longing and yearning.

The type 4 very often feels disappointed with his relationships, yet continues to wait and hope for the great love of his life to redeem him, for the noble prince or magical princess. Even if such royalty appears on the scene, bitter disappointment may quickly follow on the heels of a brief ecstatic flurry once the romance has dulled a bit and longing is no longer needed. Sometimes it seems as if the 4 type is more in love with his longing than with his actual partner. Once his longing is satisfied, he often starts seeing only the failings and shortcomings of his lover. According to Rohr and Ebert, women of the 4 type often become anorexic. In addition, the 'Emotional People' need:

> . . . friends and partners who can tolerate them without being drawn into their mood-swings. They need the experience of a partner's unshakeable faithfulness. But entering into a partnership

with an unresolved 4 type is gruelling and demands a great deal of tolerance. Since everything – including the partner – is seen as unsatisfactory, it may be that the partner is subjected to permanent, wearing criticism.[9]

The great difficulty in a relationship with a 4 type is that he is constantly testing to see whether one is doing, thinking and feeling enough for him. One has to prove one's love to him at least five times a day, or he will feel unloved.

To the Enneagram types 1 and 2, the 4 type often seems to be too hysterical and unreliable to get involved with. They are very likely outwardly to reject him, yet still be rather in awe of him in secret.

The 'Emotional Person', as his name implies, is always immediately affected by everything. He lives and stage-manages his life as a continual drama. But it is usually others who suffer; he himself finds this way of living quite normal. Any other way of life would seem dull.

In spite of his rather awesome emotionality, he is by no means weak; he knows how to invest all his strength in attaining his goals. His weakness, rather, consists of the fact that he tends to react in a wounding/wounded rage if he does not get what he wants (or if he does not get it in the way he wanted). If his aim is connected with other people, his disappointed affection can transform into feelings of deep hatred. His close connection to the emotions and to his imaginative world means that he is often very successful in artistic professions, in which he carries out his work in a very sensitive and often highly individual way. This type is often very capable of working independently. The 4 type likes being involved in unusual activities, for he likes things to be out of the ordinary: anything 'normal' is tedious beyond words.

A great obstacle to his relationships with other people is his tendency to be extremely introspective. He is likely to be much too concerned with himself, to think he is the centre of the world, and thus to overlook the needs of those around him. His unique suffering can be harnessed to tyrannize his immediate environment. This sometimes results in him losing his friends and becoming a loner. Yet he is considerably less withdrawn than Enneagram type 5. His task is to learn to balance and control his feelings.

The 4 type is usually wasteful and careless with money; for this reason it is helpful for him to look towards the 'Entrepreneur' (type 1) and try to adopt some of his thriftiness and business sense. The 'Entrepreneur's' assurance with accounts and business can often provide a harmonious balance to the 4 type's emotional roller-coaster.

The 'Planner' on the other hand, can stimulate the 4 type to uncontrolled competitiveness, since both often work in creative realms; the 'Planner' with his ambitious tendencies often gives the 'Emotional Person' the feeling of being swamped or overridden. In addition, the 'Planner' as a type representative of the first third of the Enneagram can usually react and act far quicker than the 4 type.

The 4 type's capacities for fighting, his impulsiveness and unconscious disregard of others, and also his independence, are embodied in the archetype of Aries/Mars. We should not forget that he falls under the influence of the solar plexus chakra, which helps us act in our best interests. Mars or Aries was never only a bloodthirsty warhorse, he was also a sensitive god who gave his protection to dancing and was famous as a passionate lover. The Romans thought of Mars as the father of Romulus and Remus, and as protector of their nation.

The Aries/Mars archetype guarantees this type a direct connection to his feelings, and thus also an often enviable capacity for passion. Aries/Mars is known for his spontaneity and impetuosity. He acts first and thinks later. This is a quality which frequently lands him in difficult situations. But he does usually try, at least, to control his own emotions. According to Jung he is the introverted, intuitive type, who sublimates his insecurity through art.

If types 4 and 3 combine with each other in one person, the archetype of the 'Magician' acquires a particular power through the depth of feeling of the 'Emotional Person'; and

The 'Emotional Person' or the 'Striver'

Strengths	Close connection with his feelings and spontaneity; engages himself aggressively to attain his goals; strong capacity for sexual expression
Weaknesses	Dependent on emotions; impulsive to the point of unthinking; uncontrolled outbreaks of rage, addiction to wasteful spending
Archetype	Aries/Mars
Resolved	Through Enneagram type 1, the 'Entrepreneur'; focusing on goal-orientated action and disciplined business sense has a healing effect
Hindered	By Enneagram type 2, the 'Planner'; an unhelpful competitive attitude is often released by this combination
Mixed types	4/3: harmonizing 4/5: rare combination, leading to isolation and loneliness 4/1: healing 4/2: intensifies neurosis
According to Ichazo	The misunderstood and complaining artist who is often subject to envy

his dexterity with imaginative pictures becomes still more skilled.

A negative combination, on the other hand, is that between types 4 and 5, which can often lead to a very lonely isolation from other people. Such a person will feel unloved, misunderstood and compelled to withdraw. Luckily this combination is very rare. The 4 type is basically a social being who likes best to have loved ones around him.

Type 5: The 'Observer'

The 'Observer' or the 'Sufferer' is the second of the two types who react mainly through their emotions. Like the previous type, he can also be very 'deep' and influence his immediate environment in accordance with his rich inner life. But in contrast to the 'Emotional Person', the 'Observer' is more akin to the intellect, which explains his connection to types 7 and 8. The 'Observer' actually knows a great deal and has also inwardly digested what he knows, but he experiences difficulties in applying it. We can see this from the fact that type 5's geometrical position in the Enneagram has no direct connection to the two 'action types' – numbers 1 and 2.

Through his vivid inner life and his accumulated knowledge, the 'Observer' often feels distanced from his environment, which can seem superficial and one-dimensional. This can lead him to withdraw, and, in unfavourable situations, to be sucked into a downward spiral of brooding.

The great strength of the 5 type lies in his almost natural gift for contemplation. Many great philosophers, like the Neo-Platonist Plotinus (c205–270), Thomas Aquinas (1225–1274), René Descartes (1596–1650), Ludwig Feuerbach (1804–1872) and Martin Heidegger (1889–1976), were typical 'Observers'. Like type 7, type 5 notices everything with great precision. Einstein, Nietzsche, Jean-Paul Sartre, James Joyce and Ezra Pound were all of this type according to Riso.[10] Quite an elect circle of great minds!

The 'Observer' loves to dwell upon his thoughts, memories and particularly his feelings and impressions. He tries to fill up his feeling of an inner void with his collection of emotions. But all this emotional material often burdens him, and allows him to drown in his own world. Outwardly he then often seems like an elitist who doesn't need contact with others. It is very important for this type to remind himself constantly that the human being is a 'zoon politikon' as the ancient Greeks said: a communal being, of whom a certain involvement in outer affairs, and a readiness to pull up his sleeves and get down to work is expected.

Ultimately we can recognize that he is continually striving for inner freedom, which is bound up with the power of his heart. The 'Observer' corresponds with the heart chakra (Anahata). The wisdom and freedom of his heart is easily available to him. But to live out his heart forces without any hindrance he has to overcome the shyness which makes contact with other people difficult. The type 5 usually appears controlled and timid, or shy of people. His tactic for saving himself from exposure to others consists in either becoming part of the wallpaper or hiding himself behind his (analytical) knowledge.

Love, for the type 5, is often – at least inwardly – a great drama. His closeness to the world of emotion lets him fall passionately in love. But he has, at the same time, a great need for distance and a fear of where his heart may lead him. 'Two souls dwell, alas! within my breast' (Goethe's Faust). It can often take the type 5 a long time to learn to let himself go and open himself trustingly to another. If he has received enough love and warmth as a child, he will be able to accept the affection of his partner and open his heart.

When the 'Observer' moves towards the Enneagram type 8, the 'Mediator', he will learn from him how thoughtfulness and intellect can be applied in a purposeful way to benefit society. This access to the outer world will help him become increasingly freer and more flexible. Such a combination can lead him to attain an objectivity greater than is possible for any other Enneagram type.

But if instead he focuses too much, and perhaps enviously, on the 'Optimist' (type 7), the latter's superficiality will leave him cold rather than drawing him out of his isolation.

The task of the 'Observer' is to learn how to mediate betwen his conflicting feelings, which he can do through his heart's warmth. He is a master of self-observation; which is very egocentric at the outset but can be transformed in a positive scenario into sympathy and helpfulness towards others. The attitude of the 'Observer' often has a healing effect on his environment, which is probably hectic and busy. One of his avoidance tactics therefore consists of not acting, so as not

The 'Observer' or 'Sufferer'

Strengths	Emotional depth and inner knowledge; good connection with heart forces; great capacity to heal (in all realms)
Weaknesses	Withdrawal and difficulty in taking action
Archetype	Influenced by certain aspects of Zeus/Jupiter
Resolved	Through Enneagram type 8, the 'Mediator'; combining with this type he learns both to mediate between his own contradictory feelings and also to look outwards into the society around him
Hindered	By Enneagram type 7, the 'Optimist', whose apparent superficiality he rejects, and under whose influence he experiences his inner struggles as suffering
Mixed types	5/4: emotionally one-sided 5/6: either empowering or weakening 5/7: intensifies neurosis 5/8: strongly healing
According to Ichazo	The withdrawn thinker who suffers from the purposelessness of the world

to become entangled or engaged in whatever is occurring. But he can give his friends wise pieces of advice. The 'Observer' usually feels best in a healing, research or teaching profession.

We should remember that the archetype underlying this Enneagram type is that of Zeus/Jupiter – not the Zeus as woman-chaser, but his aspect as highest divinity of the Greeks. The Jungian analyst Jean Shinoda Bolen[11] saw him as representing the 'My home is my castle' attitude. He is the sort of person who marries, makes himself a nice home, has children, and rules supreme in his little world. The 5 type needs his own space, a kingdom into which he can withdraw. It is there that he finds his strength and intuition.

In a negative scenario, that is also where he becomes something of a tyrant. However, his tendency to making the rules and 'knowing better' sometimes leads him to being emotionally remote. The depth of his own emotions can frighten him to such a degree that he prefers to hide them from others (and sometimes from himself), or even to repress them altogether. If he rules over others he does this in order to hide his feelings. He would say that it is his form of self-defence. In such situations, outsiders will be particularly aware of the 'suffering' side of the 'Observer'.

When the 'Observer' becomes more similar to the 'Emotional Person' in stress situations, an over-powerful, one-sided emotional energy is released, which distances him too much from the outside world. He himself, as well as those around him, will often take fright at this outbreak of concentrated emotional energy. He will then withdraw into himself and be exposed to the danger of exaggerated self-obsession. He becomes oversensitive, sometimes to the point of hypochondria, and loses his healing qualities.

If this type combines with the 'Hero' archetype (Enneagram type 6), he can either contribute to it a depth of experience which leads to enormous strength, or hinder it by his tendency towards withdrawal and inwardness.

Type 6: The 'Hero'

Let it be said straight away that the 'Hero' is by no means typically male: as all other Enneagram types, he manifests in both women and men.[12]

The archetype of the 'Hero' represents, without doubt, an image of the ideal human being. It clearly shows us that we are not at the mercy of blind fate, but that we can become an active and conscious shaper of ourselves and of our environment through self-contemplation and self-knowledge.

The 'Hero' knows his own emotions and tries to free himself from his anxieties, limitations and guilt feelings; he is helped in this by his tendency to forward-looking flight. He is capable of observing his shadow-sides, of accepting and thus overcoming them, and is empowered by his capacity to cope with conflict and rejection on his path towards self-realization. But he is also usually very cooperative and can work best in groups.

The 'Hero', in spite of all this, often feels as helpless in every-day life as any other Enneagram type; but he reacts to this feeling as a challenge – often too quickly or powerfully: he is sometimes too tough on himself and others. The 'Hero' must be careful not to get off on a power-trip, seeing himself as some kind of Nietzschean superman.

The 'Hero' possesses the admirable quality of going his own way with determination, patience and persistance. He may therefore seem to others a non-conformist, and thus a particularly fascinating person. Type 6 is characterized by the ability to be self-determining – a trait which many other types do not have.

But at this point of the Enneagram, serving rather than ruling has the upper hand. We find ourselves here at the conscious shock point (Enneagram point 6), where a new quality needs to enter. This new quality consists, among other things, in the challenge of serving and thus overcoming one's ego. Through service, the unconscious, mechanistic patterns of behaviour are reduced to a minimum, and free will can emerge. According to the perspective of the schools of the Fourth Way, this attitude of service is only attained when the Enneagram type 6 learns to control and so perfect himself.

His path of development goes in the direction of the 'Loving One' (type 9), who senses and knows his task and duty towards others.

In contrast to Enneagram types 4 and 5, the 'Hero' is capable of fully serving a cause. That means that he can overcome himself in his private, professional or social tasks, instead of becoming emotionally entangled in them. As long as he avoids looking too enviously towards the 'Magician' type (type 3), he will be able to observe himself and his environment objectively.

This impersonal attitude can become a problem however, if he adopts it in order to avoid getting involved with his fellow men, and to keep them at a distance. The 'Hero' easily kills off his own feelings and relies wholely on his mind, thus becoming a cold, sterile and extremely calculating and manipulating person. In this case, self-contemplation is replaced by rationality and particularly projection – which alienates the 'Hero' from himself rather than providing self-knowledge. In the worst scenario, the 'Hero' can become an anxious coward – that is, the shadow he fears.

The classical Greek hero of course possessed a solid shield which protected him from all attacks. But this shield symbolizes one's centre, rather than the place of inner withdrawal and retreat. As the German psychotherapist Lütz Müller says:

> The shield shows that the 'Hero' has found a solid but also flexible standpoint, which allows him to react with sufficient ease and forethought to attacks both from his fellow men and from the 'strokes of destiny'.13

The (psychic) shield of the 'Hero' is thus the guarantee of his flexibility and should not be viewed as a tortoise shell he withdraws into. If a 6 type uses avoidance tactics and becomes inflexible, he loses a strength natural to him: his critical awareness of reality.

In love affairs, the type 6 is an extremely faithful lover, upon whom one can rely. He supports his partner and shows solidarity with him/her. All 6 types I have been in love with had an uncomplicated approach to love: they behaved naturally and with youthful charm even at a relatively advanced age. According to the Ichazo school, the 6 types are supposed to be subject to a fear of sexuality; but in my experience this is totally untrue, though this is no doubt because I define the 6 type differently from Ichazo. One thing the 'Hero' needs to learn is to enjoy both love and life. He always reminds me of the noble Lancelot in John Steinbeck's Arthurian novel.14

Excursus: typology or path of development

The archetype of the 'Hero' is a particularly clear example of the difference between Gurdjieff's view of the Enneagram and Ichazo's typology: it is Gurdjieff's opinion that the separate points of the Enneagram represent a continuous path of development. The 'Hero' at Enneagram point 6 has already experienced the physical, material world (points 1 and 2) and purified himself through suffering and inner conflict (points 4 and 5) so that his old conditioned patterns of behaviour have been broken. He is now an individual pursuing his path. To reach Enneagram point 6, one must have passed through the preceding stages; there is no other way. According to Gurdjieff, therefore, we are not born as Enneagram types but work our way through them in the course of our lives.

According to the typology of Ichazo, on the other hand, each of the nine categories is a quite separate, independent reality. There is no continuum: type 6 is not more developed than types 1 or 2. We are, therefore, born more or less as one type, which is then reinforced by the – usually unconscious – process of socialization. Each type possesses its own strengths and weaknesses, which are not dependent on the other types.

There is also a wide divergence between the qualities attributed to the different types by Ichazo, and those attributed in my system based on Gurdjieff. According to Ichazo, the 6 type is pervaded by self-doubt and is emotionally highly dependent on other people. This fundamentally contradicts the Gurdjieffian view that at point 6 we become independent individuals possessing free will. In the Ichazo tradition, the 6 type is often called the 'notorious loser'. The fear cited by Ichazo as this type's chief characteristic, is, according to Gurdjieff, overcome at precisely this point, so that the way opens for a new, undreamed-of potential for freedom.

Enneagram type 6 is for Gurdjieff a new qualitative leap in the Enneagram system, since free will now enters the picture. For Ichazo, this type has no such special characteristics. He does not recognize the qualitative differences between types, nor the evolutionary steps which belong to them.

The 'Hero'

Strengths	Objective observation of himself and his environment; the courage to go his own way in spite of outer obstacles; will-power
Weaknesses	A tendency to observe his surroundings from a distance; pride and obsession with power; rationalization of feelings
Resolved	Through Enneagram type 9, the 'Loving One'; the perspective towards this archetype opens his heart
Hindered	By Enneagram type 3, the 'Magician'; looking towards this archetype tempts him to embark on power-trips
According to Ichazo	The anxious and doubting person

As an aspect of personality present in all of us, or as one among a number of different egos, I view the 'Hero', like Ichazo, as being no more nor less developed than the other Enneagram types. Yet I try to retain a flexibility and openness in my understanding of the typology which allows me to see it both as a system of types of equal value *and* as an evolutionary continuum. It is up to the reader and his own approach to decide which of these points of view he prefers to adopt. In the strictest Gurdjieffian sense, we would do better to forget the attribution of certain types to the various Enneagram points, since this induces us to act mechanistically and associatively, instead of with conscious intelligence.

My typology is based on a compromise in which two different concepts intersect: that of nine different egos, and that of the evolutionary process from type 1 to 9. In this latter process the number of egos diminishes as we evolve; and from point 6 we become one ego, and thus an independent individual.

But let us return to the 'Hero' himself, who represents the first mind or intellectual type in the system. The 'Observer' (Enneagram point 5) knew a thing or two, but his view and experience was largely emotional. The 'Hero', on the other hand, can distance himself from his emotions and observe them 'objectively', without identifying with them. He is therefore no longer swayed by mood-swings, and can pursue his goal in a focused way.

Type 7: The 'Optimist'

The 'Optimist' or 'Teacher' possesses a gift for quick understanding, which enables him to gain an overview of all possible aspects of everyday life. The archetype of Uranos/Uranus is at work in the 'Optimist', giving him a great dynamism and power to make decisions. One can accuse him of a certain superficiality, but he balances this with his flexibility and versatility. The Enneagram type 7 is the typical 'information storer' who can come out with a particular piece of information when it's called for. He accumulates experiences and almost immediately forgets or represses their negative aspects, since he does not wish to suffer.

I myself am a type 7. My therapist had to show me that I had formed an unrealistically positive image of my life story, based on a wholesale repression of all wounding experiences. When I first came into contact with a teacher of the Fourth Way, he asked me – to my absolute horror – whether I wanted to remain a simple smiling boy all my life. Of course I wanted to! He then asked me about any emotional hurts I had received – and, typically, none came to mind. 'If you wish to grow up', he said, 'you must realize that your world is not all wonderful fun, and sweetness and light.' I was, of course, indignant and looked around for a 'better teacher'. It was not until much later that I understood how much sadness was hidden beneath my laughing exterior, and how many amusing stories I had invented about my life – although disappointment and deep wounds remained below the surface. I had to draw on all my reserves of courage to avoid giving everything a happy or comic twist. Five years ago I wrote this Irish saying into my diary as a motto: 'Why spoil a good story by telling the truth?' Much of what I, as a 7 type, undertake, is done in order to flee my deep inner pain. The 7 type is often accused of being 'addicted to the adrenalin-rush'; and that certainly applies to me. At least three times a day I need my fix of excitement and euphoria; otherwise life seems like the slough of despond! I always want to be cheerful rather than sad; I want to enjoy the sunny side of life!

One of the great strengths of the 7 type is that he can present himself and the fruits of his work in an easy-going way – often with a touch of eroticism – to the outside world. His Achilles' heel is his immeasurable ambition, which often leads him to identify totally with his work and personality. This is, according to Gurdjieff, a great weakness. The developed person treats his work as play, and does not identify with it too strongly. This identification with our work makes us highly dependent on success and failure; we thus easily lose our own centre and stability and are at the mercy of our feelings.

This Enneagram type is very suited to being a teacher; he can enthuse and transport his pupils. But some people of this type look on the teaching profession as too little of a challenge. Nevertheless they often spend a good deal of time giving the people around them a lesson or lecture or two; thank goodness in an amusing and entertaining way.

Since the 'Optimist' is an intellectually orientated type, he likes getting involved in all sorts of research and investigation – as long as it does not look inwards! Despite his thoughtfulness, he retains the 'beginner' attitude of the type 1, and often seems like the eternal student. According to Jung, the archetype of the eternal youth or maiden is permeated with fascination about his or her own origins. Such people do not want to wave goodbye to their state of childhood, but would prefer always to be growing up. The Jung follower Marie-Louise von Franz sees the most pronounced aspect of this archetype in an overemphasis on the intellect.[15] In spite of his intellect, which ought to protect him from pain, the 7 type tends to be greedy for things. He is certainly at risk from addictions; he wants to enjoy life, to drain it to the very dregs – and drinks, smokes, eats and talks too much.

In stress situations, the 'Optimist' may draw closer to the 'Entrepreneur' (Enneagram type 1), which pressurizes him and easily turns him into a workaholic.

What he needs is to internalize his experiences; to look towards the 'Observer' (type 5), who, in spite of a certain intellectualism, has a strong relationship to his heart forces. The 'Optimist' tends to neglect his feeling life, because it seems to him to be a muddled confusion which gets in his way. In addition he is so speedy that one experience follows quickly on the heels of another and he has no time to internalize them. The Enneagram type 7 is usually very fast, nervous and easily excitable.

It is typical of the 'Optimist' that he can easily and speedily make relationships and has many friends with whom he is on very good, easy-going terms. A 7 type seldom allows himself to be pinned down; he is as flexible, fluid and slippery as the intellect which shapes him.

To the 'Optimist' corresponds the throat chakra (Vishuddha), the energy centre which rules human communication. He is definitely the most communicative type. For him, the path to the other leads – just as the Hassidic philosopher Martin Buber (1878–1965) expressed it – through conversation. In addition to his love of dialogue, the 'Optimist' has an erotic charisma and a close relationship to his sexuality, which he considers the most intense form of communication. Like the Enneagram type 4, the type 7 is almost always a good, imaginative and playful lover. He does not carry around a heavy burden of sexual taboos.

In bed, the 7 type almost always prefers the easy, perhaps even uncommitted play of sex and eroticism to earth-shaking and dramatic passion. In love, as in life, the 7 type needs his adventures and his erotic escapades. The film director Milos Foreman, in his film about Mozart, quite clearly depicted the latter's coquetterie and erotic fancifulness. Mozart is a classic example of a genuine 7 type.

The 'Optimist' or 'Teacher'

Strengths	Communication; versatility; quick intellectual grasp of situations; circumspection
Weaknesses	Disregards his emotionality; rejects and suppresses negative experiences, especially suffering; narcissism
Archetype	Uranos/Uranus
Resolved	Through Enneagram type 5, the 'Observer', which gives him more peace and profundity
Hindered	By Enneagram type 1, the 'Entrepreneur', which easily turns him into a workaholic
Mixed types	7/6: often intensifies neurosis, since the power-drive of the 'Hero' is emphasized 7/8: either too one-sidedly intellectual or an ideal server of a cause, task or idea 7/1: intensifies neurosis 7/5: healing, since his heart forces are strengthened
According to Ichazo	The greedy, hungry child

One of the 'Optimist's' greatest tasks is to learn to recognize that sacrifice of some kind is necessary to attain a goal or to nurture a relationship. The idea of sacrifice and of the suffering connected with it is anathema to this type. He derives his sunny self-confidence through an (apparent) circumspection, which makes a strange contrast to his youthful audacity. But his distance from his feelings lets him react optimistically to all possible situations. This circumspection and intellectualism is usually driven by a deep fear of losing control of a situation, thus plunging into chaos.

If the 'Optimist' combines with the 'Hero' archetype (Enneagram type 6), the tendency of the 'Hero' to rationalize his feelings can often be reinforced. Such a person will therefore seem manipulative, but also has the power to enthuse others for his ideas.

When the 'Optimist' and the 'Mediator' (Enneagram type 8) combine, such a person can either throw himself into serving a task or cause in a wonderful way, or react too intellectually to himself and his surroundings.

Type 8: The 'Mediator'

According to Gurdjieff, the one who stands at Enneagram point 8 has reached his goal and becomes wholly one with it. In the schools of the Fourth Way it is said that one develops a living soul at points 7 and 8.

The 'Mediator' wholly sacrifices himself to his task and grows beyond the limitations of his own ego. The Enneagram type 8 represents a transpersonal stage of self-development, in which one can harmonize all one's forces and become, as humanistic psychology puts it, a fully-evolved human being.

This type knows all about emotional suffering (Enneagram point 5) and is capable of dealing and playing around with the material side of life (Enneagram point 2). At this point, the inner connecting lines of the Enneagram unite the three highest levels of all three sections (Enneagram point 2 in the material and Enneagram point 5 in the emotional realms). The Enneagram type 7, in comparison, is at a lower stage of spiritual and emotional development.

The shadow of the 'Mediator', however, consists in the fact that he has lost his naïvety and innocence (whereas the type 7, for instance, still preserves this to a large degree). The loss of innocence often allows him to become jealous and dismissive towards people who go through life in a naïve, optimistic way. Teachers of the Fourth Way are often 'Mediators', which is why such groups are often so unrelievedly earnest, reasonable and heavy-going that you start to feel suffocated. The frequent near-absurdity of Gurdjieff's sense of humour is something quite alien to this Enneagram type.

I once encountered a typical example of this sort of weightiness at a meal during a meeting of English Gurdjieff groups: the chief teacher overseeing the occasion suddenly ordained, in words laden with significance, that we might all now enjoy ouselves and be merry! At that point I nearly choked on my mouthful.

Gurdjieff himself had a well-developed, surrealistic sense of humour, that comes to the fore particularly in *Beelzebub's Tales To His Grandson*. After all, he grew up familiar with Mullah Nasrudin's tales (called by Gurdjieff: Mullah Nassr Eddin).[16] In Gurdjieff's works he can be seen as the embodiment of a healthy tradition of folk wisdom and traditional humour.

Rohr and Ebert[17] regard Gurdjieff as a typical type 8. He embodies the fighting aspect of this type, someone who never gives in and always reacts immediately to every 'error' of his opponent. Gurdjieff and Madame Jeanne de Salzmann always emphasized the need for fighting – but, at the same time, for distancing oneself from the conflict rather than getting involved and bogged down in it. The 8 type loves playing the role of angry young man or woman. He can be a real *enfant terrible*. In *Life Is Real Only Then, When I Am*, Gurdjieff describes how he undertook to find the Achilles' heel or weakest spot of every person he encountered. He was known and feared for relentlessly walking roughshod on the problems of his pupils, which became an important part of his method. Such an aggressive approach helped enormously, though, to develop his pupils' potential. And that is precisely what is an important characteristic of this type – that he has an enormous capacity for leading others to their own – often unrecognized – potential.

If we examine the 'Mediator' in the schema of equal-ranking Enneagram types, we will see that he has a great ability for mediating between very different opinions and people; and that he has a feeling for how to go about settling disputes. He is good at this because he does not identify too closely with his own emotions; he therefore does not feel a need to make value judgements and can thus remain relatively neutral. The 'Mediator' is a reasonable person who is firmly rooted in real life. He knows what he wants and is also prepared to do everything in his power to attain his goal.

Friendships are very important indeed for the Enneagram type 8. He is prepared to sacrifice himself for his cause and for his friends, if this should prove necessary.[18] The 'Mediator' feels happy when he has a clique around him and in which he is, preferably, the focus, for he does not easily develop trust in other people. He often acts from a position of high principles

The 'Mediator'

Strengths	Capacity for mediating, even in difficult situations; relatively neutral attitude towards his own feelings; very active in support of his ideals and friends
Weaknesses	Fear of his own unconscious, and of suffering; fear of confronting himself; in negative situations can show envy and bitterness; desire for ruling others
Archetype	Poseidon/Neptune
Resolved	Through Enneagram type 2, the 'Planner', which intensifies his creative powers
Hindered	By Enneagram type 5, the 'Observer', who makes him more anxious and fearful
Mixed types	8/2: healing 8/5: activates neurotic fears 8/7: tendency to a one-sided, intellectual approach 8/9: healing
According to Ichazo	A powerful fighter for his ideals

and ideals, which also informs all his friendships. He finds it almost impossible to come adrift from his ideals or to change them. This can make him appear rigid and boring, but also gives him the strength to reach his goal.

Like the type 7, the 'Mediator' is an extrovert, who blossoms in a circle of friends. He is also usually a family man or woman, and knows how to use his social skills to avoid almost all family conflict. But he does not withdraw into the bosom of his family; he loves throwing parties and being at the centre of warm social gatherings.

It is important for this type to have well-ordered finances. If this does not happen – which is unusual – his outgoing confidence can backfire into devouring envy and deep unhappiness. This type fears nothing more than weakness and failure.

In sexual matters he is either astonishingly conservative and prudish, or uses sexuality as power, to gain possession of his partner. This sort of man and woman will try to control the other by alternating between sexual enticement and withdrawal. Such a type is also representative of the coy virgin and the engaged couple – as one might find them in a Barbara Cartland novel. The sexual aspect of this type is ruled by ideals and power.

If you experience sexual difficulties with an 8 type you can be quite sure that it will seem to be all your fault. Both in life and in bed, the 'Mediator' always makes out the other to be in the wrong. He is a master of 'projection', who will not stop at any falsehood in order to assert his ascendency.

The 8 type's major problem is that he doesn't like dealing with his feelings. For this reason he must always seem to be in command. He also doesn't like being alone: the withdrawn attitude of the 5 type scares him – though he would never show or admit to fear, even to himself. He loses all his imagination and creativity if he has to spend a long time without a partner and friends.

Since he is influenced by the Poseidon/Neptune archetype, he is very susceptible to fear of his dark, unconscious powers. This fear is responsible for his failure to identify with his feelings; in contrast to the 'Emotional Person' (type 4), he likes to avoid dramatic upsets and tumult at all costs.

If the 'Mediator' looks towards the 'Observer' (Enneagram type 5), all this fear of loneliness, and the darkness in his soul, rises up in him. It is therefore easier and more natural for him to keep his sights trained on the 'Planner' or 'Shaper' (type 2). He connects with the type 2 through his creative, active aspect, which represents the strength of both these types.

Another natural combination is with the type 7, since both are not only extrovert but also capable, usually, of getting a firm grip on their life.

Type 9: The 'Loving One'

According to Gurdjieff, Ouspensky and Bennett, and more or less all esoteric schools, love is the power which ultimately sustains all life processes. It binds and welds together the active and passive energies at work in the world. The schools of the Fourth Way say that at point 9 of the Enneagram one becomes open for new tasks. At its culminating apex, a process makes the transition into something new – into a new Enneagram in fact.

If we look upon the baseline of the equilateral triangle – between Enneagram points 3 and 6 – as the Enneagram's feeling aspect, then the 'Loving One' represents the intensification or culmination of this. The sort of love meant is of course unconditional – a force which all esoteric groups invoke. Such a force, in the view of the English medium Eileen Caddy, is particularly manifest in Findhorn, a large spiritual community and Mystery School in the North of Scotland.

The Tarot has a trump card, 'The Lovers', which calls forth the need for a decision and thus for entering into dedication to a task. 'The Lovers' are a symbol of lost and regained paradise, for Enneagram point 9 has a double function: it is both the end and the new beginning of the Enneagram; it is the nine which ends the process, and the zero with which a new one begins.

At the zero point we enter the Enneagram and into the

differentiation between nine different types, because we have fallen out of a state of unity (love or paradise). Once we have developed through the nine Enneagram points we can rediscover this lost wholeness at a new level.

In the Enneagram typology, the 'Loving One' must be characterized as an introverted feeling type. But it is important to rememember that we are concerned here with love, not with falling in love, which renders us blind, as we know. Love is a mature, evolved outlook, informed by sympathy and solidarity, which is lacking in the dramas of romance. Falling in love has very little to do with Enneagram point 9: it is largely characterized by idealistic projections, whereas love consists in seeing beyond them.

The 'Loving One' represents the sluggish and passive type of the Enneagram. To him is attributed a tendency to laziness. He loves his peace and quiet and often becomes very dependent on his partner. In rare cases he can become dependent on his work.

In matters of love, the 9 type is lazy to the extent that he will never actively free himself from a relationship. It is always the other who finishes it. The 9 type will only end a partnership in the sense that he withdraws completely into himself and becomes inaccessible. In a sexual affair, he can, like the 3 type, accommodate himself easily to every partner, though in his case this can take on the form of complete submission.

This dependency, which can wholly enrage the type 7, does not much bother the 'Loving One'; it actually seems to give him security. He needs this to develop his desire, and in the right circumstances can radiate an astonishing sexual attraction. In his own ordered realm the 'Loving One' is a happy person, who only explodes in very threatening situations – unless he chooses instead to keep his head down and endure stoically and passively. The 9 type is simply an endearing person, who makes a humble and modest impression, although he knows how to turn his passive aggression to good advantage.

The 'Loving One' is by no means inclined to throw himself into the service of an idea or task. He much prefers to sit quietly within the four walls of his usually pleasant, comfortable house and enjoy the peaceful atmosphere. He likes to sip a glass of wine in these homely surroundings, perhaps also to smoke a joint, and he's happy if 'God's in his heaven and all's right with the world'! The motto of this type is: 'Keep everything light'.

The four extrovert types of the Enneagram (1, 2, 7 and 8) can find a source of great healing from establishing contact with the 'Loving One'. Unfortunately, though, they usually either find him boring or don't notice him at all.

The 'Loving One' is frequently underestimated because of his passivity. In fact he has attained the wisdom of inaction or non-intervention. This is the frame of mind which the ancient Chinese called Wu-wei and regarded very highly. To reach this point it is necessary to stop identifying with one's own ego – in striking contrast to the 'Entrepreneur' and the 'Planner' (types 1 and 2). However, this is not to say that the 'Loving One' consciously adopts this attitude. If he does, though, he can really be regarded as the most highly evolved type of the Enneagram. In this case he represents the fulfilment of the nine-point process.

The Ichazo school regards C G Jung as an individual strongly influenced by Enneagram type 9. Jung's life-task can be seen as a striving to integrate everything: the great *Coniunctio* (fusion or merging), which unites male and female, good and evil, spirit and matter, plays a major role in his analytical system. He discovered the integrating force of the collective unconscious. Many people of this Enneagram type are very gifted; but in contrast to Jung, they often – through laziness – fail to develop their talents, which then slumber on undiscovered within them.

If the 'Loving One' fails to develop ego strength – that is, in psychoanalytical terms, if he remains an oral-dependent type (a kind of narcissism) – then he occupies a position at the beginning of the Enneagram, at the zero point as it were. It is then his task to involve himself with the world and its processes; he can be helped in this by looking towards the 'Magician'

The 'Loving One'

Strengths	Content with his love; diminishment of ego – letting things happen; not getting involved
Weaknesses	Passivity and laziness
Resolved	Through Enneagram type 3, the 'Magician', who leads him towards a connection with his surroundings; healing influences from types 1 and 8
Hindered	By Enneagram type 6, the 'Hero', who reinforces his tendency to distance himself from the outer world
According to Ichazo	The lazy genius

(Enneagram type 3), who takes pleasure in dealing with the material elements of the world.

The 'Hero' (Enneagram type 6), on the other hand, who has a tendency to rationalize his feelings, would only reinforce the sluggishness of the type 9; even more so because the 'Hero' likes to keep himself at a distance from his surroundings.

A combination with either the 'Entrepreneur' (type 1) or the 'Mediator' (type 8) has a vitalizing and also healing, balancing effect on the 'Loving One' archetype.

The striking thing about this archetype is that his love is sufficient for him. He does not need to sublimate anything by means of work and achievement. As Bertolt Brecht said: 'To lovers love's the stopping place . . . '

Gurdjieff's character typologies

Whether you wish to see these nine Enneagram types as an evolutionary process or as separate, equal-value types depends on your interests, the way in which you want to use the Enneagram, and what you want to apply it to. If you wish to observe your various egos and understand yourself better in relation to other people and specific situations, it will be useful to see the types as distinct and equal. Such an approach can clearly demonstrate to you the unbalanced ways in which you react, and also which egos it would be good to activate to counteract this.

But if you are more interested in how you can systematically develop and fulfill yourself; if, therefore, you are interested in pursuing an esoteric path, you can see the typology as a path of evolution from point 1 to point 9.

The path of psychology is paved with character typologies. Galen's 2nd-century theory of the four temperaments was one of the first. The German philosopher Immanuel Kant (1724–1804) drew extensively upon it. In modern times we have the systems of Freud, Jung and Eysenck, to name only the best known.

It should also be mentioned that Gurdjieff himself also propounded a typology that was largely disregarded. It distinguishes seven kinds of people according to their degree of consciousness.

Type 1: is the sleeping or automatic person, whose focal point lies in in his motor centre. His knowledge depends upon instinct and imitation. I call this first type the body-orientated person. The Indian author Bhagwan Sri Rajneesh, drawing on Gurdjieff, says of this type that he doesn't eat to live but lives to eat. He is under the body's enchantment. If this type of person comes to a party, he says to himself, more or less unconsciously: 'Here I am; now all of you come and take an interest in me.' He relies on being able to 'tune in' to a given situation, and reacts spontaneously and instinctively to the attitudes he encounters in others.

Type 2: is the sleeping person whose focus is his feelings. His view of the world is determined by his emotional acceptance or rejection of things. He always desires things to be pleasant and tends towards sentimentality; he is often blinded by his feelings.

When invited to a party, the greatest issue for him is whether the other guests like him and find him attractive or whether they reject him.

Type 3: is the sleeping person whose focus is his thoughts. His view of the world depends upon his own subjectively logical thinking which blinds him. At a party he will spontaneously adopt a distant attitude, and from this standpoint interest himself in what is going on there and how the guests are relating to one another.

These three types are unaware and inattentive; they go blindly through life and know neither their goal nor their origin. To find out which of the three applies to you, I would advise you to keep a diary for a week, writing down in it what most preoccupies you. Just write what you have spent most of your day doing, and what your fantasies were mostly concerned with. This will show you quite clearly which of these three types you belong to.

Type 4: is the awoken person (here we have a qualitative leap). If one is born as a type 1, 2 or 3, one can only become a type 4 through one's own efforts. This type is on the path towards objective knowledge. He represents a transitional stage.

The previously described nine Enneagram types only appear in the first four of Gurdjieff's seven types. From the fifth of his types onwards, wholeness has been attained, and the limitations and constraints of the first four types, upon which Ichazo's typology rests, have been overcome.

Type 5: is a person who has achieved unity of personality and possesses an indivisible ego. His knowledge is an integrated whole of all three centres (motor, feeling and intellect).

Type 6: is a fully evolved person, but his characteristics are not yet stable. He possesses a consciousness, a will, an unalterable ego and individuality.

Type 7: has attained everything which the type 6 attained; but he can no longer lose his knowledge and individuality. Another difference is that while the type 6 has evolved fully, there is no longer such a thing as self-evolution for the type 7. He is beyond all such concepts and points of view.

It is possible to attribute these seven types to different points of the Enneagram, although Gurdjieff himself never did this. It is a little problematic, because the first three Gurdjieff types must be 'housed' in the first two Enneagram types; then there is a qualitative leap, and in the second Enneagram section the Gurdjieff types 4 and 5 would correspond to the Enneagram types 4 and 5. Then comes a further qualitative leap: full evolution is attained, and the Gurdjieff types 6 and 7 can be assigned to the Enneagram points 7 and 8 of the third section. However, the fact that the first two Enneagram points have to have the first three types 'crammed into them' rather unsettles an otherwise very illuminating sytem.

The Enneagram typology possesses a special dynamic quality which clearly demonstrates the interrelationship of individual types to each other; and at the same time also has a holistic overview of the complete evolving process – a view, one could say, of cosmic harmony.

The Enneagram shows, for example, how types, colours, planets and the energy centres of the human body relate to one another, and thus clearly evokes the parallelism which exists between the different realms and aspects of our world. The connections between the microcosm (of the human ego for example) and the macrocosm (the planets), become, in the Enneagram, far more than an abstract concept: the actual details of these interrelationships come into focus. The Enneagram thus offers us a map by means of which we can find our way in the world. The other typologies I am familiar with do not do this.

Notes

1   Gurdjieff quoted by Ouspensky, P D, *In Search of the Miraculous*.

2   Ouspensky, P D, *In Search of the Miraculous*.

3   Reich, Wilhelm, *Character Analysis*.

4   Jaxon-Bear, Eli, *Die neun Zahlen des Lebens: Das Enneagram – Charakterfixierung und spirituelles Wachstum*.

5   Rohr, Richard and Ebert, Andreas, *Discovering the Enneagram. An Ancient Tool, a new spiritual journey*. This is a very theologically orientated book, which has little to do with the spirit of Gurdjieff.

6   Riso, Richard, *Personality Types: Using the Enneagram for Self-Discovery*.

7   Rohr, R, and Ebert: A. *Discovering the Enneagram*.

8   Fromm, Erich, *To Have or To Be*.

9   Rohr, R, and Ebert, A, *Discovering the Enneagram*.

10 Riso, R, *Personality Types*.

11 Bolen, Jean Shinoda, *Gods in Everyman: a new psychology of men's lives and loves*.

12 It was Gurdjieff's point of view that women already know everything but need the right man to develop further. Men, on the other hand, have to learn everything from scratch, and with the right woman can find their way more speedily.

13 Müller, Lütz: *Der Held. Jeder ist dazu geboren*.

14 Steinbeck, John, *Acts of King Arthur and His Noble Knights*.

15 Cf in regard to men: Franz, Marie-Louise von, *Puer Aeternus: a psychological study of the adult struggle*; and in regard to women (although such studies are still in their infancy): Leonard, Linda, *Töchter und Väter. Heilung und Chancen einer verletzten Beziehung*.

16 Cf Moore, J, *Gurdjieff: The Anatomy of a Myth*, page 9. Mullah Nasrudin is the wise fool of Turkish tradition, who almost invariably upsets our normal view of things. Nasrudin can also be seen as a personification of paradox. He is the jovial anti-hero whose supposed grave Gurdjieff visited in Akskehir in 1885.

17 Rohr, R, and Ebert, A, *Discovering the Enneagram*.

18 Friedrich Schiller gave very beautiful expression to this attitude of the Enneagram type 8, in his famous poem 'Die Bürgschaft' (The Pledge).

CHAPTER 5

Colours in the Enneagram

> . . . as far as the 'law of colour combination' is concerned, all the traditional knowledge about it was continually passsed down from generation to generation, getting more and more degenerate every year, until – two hundred years ago – it was wholly forgotten.
>
> *G I Gurdjieff*

Gurdjieff, Ouspensky and Bennett believed that the Enneagram embodied all life processes. Goethe and Rudolf Steiner thought the sequence of the colour spectrum in the colour circle was a reflection of the whole range of life processes. When the German hero Faust sees a rainbow, at the beginning of the second part of Goethe's play, he calls out joyfully: 'In coloured reflection is life given to us.'[1]

If the Enneagram and the colours can illustrate life processes for us, then the Enneagram should also be capable of clarifying the laws of the colour circle. But Gurdjieff thought – I must come clean about this – that our present knowledge about colour and light is a lot of nonsense. It is my feeling that he overlooked the real struggle for knowledge which the colour theory represents. Goethe arrived at such a deep knowledge of colour that he was able to exert a healthy opposition to Newton's positivistic approach. One must also remember that it wasn't until after Gurdjieff's death that the importance of colour was recognized in almost all religious movements; and that in new therapies, particularly humanistic therapies, a new knowledge and deep understanding of colour came about through intensive observation of its phenomena.

Colours, alongside sounds and tones, are the most important element of our sense-world. Since the Enneagram is a model capable of clarifying the structure of the colour circle, as well as the vibrations and relationships of colours with each other, and because this aspect has been ignored in all previous Enneagram studies, I wish now to devote a chapter to this subject.

The Enneagram was originally modelled on the laws under-lying music and tone, so it is understandable that the musical aspect of the Enneagram was emphasized by Ouspensky. He drew attention to the pattern of the octave and the two half-tone steps, which were equated with the two shock points. Ouspensky continually referred to this musical correspondence in all his written works, and therefore it does not specially need to be repeated now.

But if we look upon the colours as, in Goethe's phrase, 'the joys and sufferings of the light', the colour Enneagram can offer us a diagram that shows us light's qualitative stages.

Colour attribution 1

The corners of the triangle, the Enneagram points 3, 6 and 9, form the shock points at which new qualities enter the system. These three qualities correspond to the three primary colours which represent the colour world's basis and origin. They cannot be made from other colours; but all other colours can be derived from them.

The world of colours is composed, basically, from the polarity between *blue* and *yellow*, in which blue represents the darkness and yellow the light. This polarity would allow us to allocate blue to *Enneagram point 3*, and yellow to *Enneagram point 6*. The path from the one to the other is also therefore that between darkness and light, which is what we earlier ascertained about these two points: here we encounter doubt and suffering on the path towards clarity. We struggle our way through to the light of consciousness, which is symbolized in colour psychology as the primary colour yellow. This colour radiates, thus overcoming every barrier, as does the spirit.[2] The painters and Bauhaus teachers Wassily Kandinsky, Paul Klee and Johannes Itten thought that a yellow triangle was a perfect symbol for the spirit.

It is noticeable that Gurdjieff, in his brilliant work *Beelzebub's Tales to His Grandson*, like Goethe in his *Theory of Colours*, took the struggles between light and dark as his starting point. In his ballet, *The Struggle of the Magicians*,[3] that was never publicly performed but which Gurdjieff constantly rehearsed, the white forces of light are set in opposition to the black forces of darkness. In Gurdjieff's system we can also attribute light and dark to sun and moon. Yellow is the power of the sun and of consciousness, possessing a free, focused will and highly concentrated attention and awareness. Blue is the power of the moon, and symbolic of the pulling forces of the unconscious, of egotism, lies, susceptibility to others' influence and a permanent state of sleep. Also relevant is the fact that blue in a painting or landscape always fades away into the distance, while yellow conquers the foreground.

Blue, at Enneagram point 3, symbolizes – as the colour of the deep ocean and the high dome of the sky – the soul or feeling centre. At the mechanical shock point (point 3), the psyche or emotions enter the system as a new quality. In colour psychology terms, the pure retreating blue represents our emotions or the ground of the soul; which is why the cloak of Mary, the mother of God, is traditionally always depicted as blue.

At the conscious shock point (point 6) the spirit enters the process as a new quality, to which yellow is attributed. Gabriel, the archangel of the Annunciation, is always traditionally painted yellow.

Enneagram points 4 and 5 thus lie between these two polarities and are to be thought of as *green* – a colour which Rudolf Steiner said represented the 'dead image of life'. Green is of course formed from a mixture of blue, the colour of darkness, and yellow, that of light. The doubt (Harnelahut) we can experience on a progression between the two polarities exactly corresponds to this combination of light and dark. Consciousness and the unconscious, spirit and emotions, battle within our soul just as light and dark do in the world of colour. This inner struggle constrains us, and our life does not yet have an open path before it. This is why Rudolf Steiner and the anthroposophists consider green to be the 'dead image of life'. Life itself is still missing, and will only come into play at point 6 when a uniting consciousness is attained.

Pure or bright *red* (called magenta by printers) – which Goethe called crimson in his colour theory[4] – represents an intensification or sublimation of the blue/yellow polarity. Yellow intensifies through orange, and blue through violet, to red. Red must therefore be placed in our colour Enneagram at the apex, *Enneagram point 9*. There is thus a natural ordering of colour dynamics, of the polarity blue/yellow and its intensification red, to the equilateral triangle of the Enneagram.

In the warm pole of the spectrum lies the mixed colour *orange*. Asiatic monks are very fond of dressing in this colour. The warm orange, in colour psychology, is connected with sympathy. And it is precisely this quality which characterizes *Enneagram points 7 and 8*, at which we attain our self-chosen goal. The symbolic language of colours shows us unmistakeably that we can only attain our aim when we learn to emanate warmth and sympathy towards other people and our surroundings. This is a form of wisdom which plays a particularly important role in both Buddhism and Christianity. Gautama Buddha's actions were determined by love and sympathy. In Christian tradtion, sympathy is seen as a form of compassion (or sharing others' suffering).

Enneagram points 1 and 2 are connected with the colour *violet*. This is a mixture of red, symbolic of the body, and blue, symbolic of darkness and the unconscious; and is also a colour that is very dependent on illumination from without. According to the available degree of brightness – either daylight or artificial light – the same tone of violet can appear as anything from neutral grey to shimmering red or blue. It was for this reason that violet was very unpopular as a colour for clothes up to the 20th century. Art nouveau, and later the women's movement, made violet fashionable.

So violet, with its typical instability, precisely characterizes the beginning of a path or process: the body reacts to every influence in an unconscious or automatic manner, without being able to hold a straight, purposeful course. It is only with violet's complementary colour, yellow, that a focused and directed will-power allows us to pursue our aims.

In the Enneagram, the cold colours are on the right-hand side, the warm ones on the left. Proceeding from point 1 to point 6 we make a journey from darkness into light. This journey begins with the dark colour violet; from there we develop in the direction of yellow, the colour of knowledge and consciousness. Once we have attained this knowledge and its accompanying relative state of awareness, we can further evolve and intensify towards greater mastery, towards the colour red in other words. From point 6 to point 9 we proceed through an intensification from yellow to red. The Enneagram, like the colour theory of the Bauhaus that was influenced by Goethe, divides colours into three qualities.

- From *Enneagram point 1 to Enneagram point 3* we find the cold and dark colours. They arise from darkness. In nature we perceive them when we look towards darkness through a side-illuminated mist or cloudiness. (That is why the sky seems blue: we are gazing upon the blackness of the cosmos through the sun-illumined atmosphere.)
- From *Enneagram point 6 to Enneagram point 8* the warm, bright colours appear. They derive from the light. We perceive them in nature when we look towards the light through a thinner or thicker veil of cloud or atmosphere. That is why the the sun appears red behind the smoke from a bonfire, but yellow through the atmosphere's lesser density.
- The three *Enneagram points 4, 5 and 9* correspond to the two 'intermediate' colours green and red (complementary or

opposite colours to each other). Red is formed from a combination of the intensification of yellow (orange-red) and
blue (violet-red). Green is formed from the actual combination of yellow and blue.

The complementary colours[5] are also determined in this system
by the fact that, as with yellow and its complementary violet,
blue and its complementary orange, red and its complementary
green, they are not connected by Enneagram lines. This ordering of the colours comes about through the fact that the three
primary colours occupy the corners of the triangle, and the
three secondary colours (those made by mixing the primary
colours) are assigned to the six hexagram points. Since the
triangle and the hexagram are unconnected in the Enneagram,
the primary and secondary colours, and also the complementary
colours, must likewise be unconnected by diagram lines, for a

Figure 29 *The colours in the Enneagram (1)*

complementary colour pair always consists of a primary colour and the corresponding secondary colour.

It is characteristic of this colour Enneagram that the primal or chief energies – the primary colours – are to be found at the triangle corners, while the derived energies, which are formed by mixing different combinations of the primary colours, are assigned to the hexagram points. We thus arrive at the following division of the six colours in the Enneagram shown in the table below.

The colour-polarity between light (yellow) and darkness (blue) corresponds in the Enneagram to the transition we call

	Colour	**Quality**
Enneagram points 1 and 2	Violet	dark, cold, active colour of darkness
Enneagram point 3	BLUE, primary colour (soul, the unconscious	dark, active colour of darkness, the cold pole of the spectrum
Enneagram points 4 and 5	Green	intermediate, inactive mixture of light and darkness
Enneagram point 6	YELLOW, primary colour (spirit, consciousness)	bright, active colour of light, the warm pole of the spectrum
Enneagram points 7 and 8	Orange	bright, warm, inactive colour of light
Enneagram point 9	RED, primary colour (body, matter)	intermediate, inactive, the product of the intensification of yellow and blue

the 'Night Sea Voyage of the Hero' (see page 69). Red, as the ideal bright colour, which occupies a position exactly midway between warm and cold, and between light and dark, is the uniting power which holds sway at Enneagram point 9.

This allocation of colours in the Enneagram makes sharp distinctions between primary and secondary colours, and is built up on their interrelationships and mixture potentials.

Colour attribution 2

There is another useful way of assigning colours of the spectrum to the Enneagram points. This shows how dynamic and flexible the Enneagram can be: it can usually sustain several different possible solutions, which often reveal a variety of different underlying laws; we can see things in a number of various ways, with differing emphases and from different standpoints.

The second system emphasizes the perspective towards complementary colours in the colour circle. The colour red (Goethe's crimson), is assigned to point 1; so red is, suitably, seen as the colour of beginning, or as the mother of all colours.[6] This position of red is obtained naturally when I orientate the three points of the triangle exactly towards the three transition points between secondary and primary colours in the colour circle. *Figure 30* demonstrates this.

It is the perspectives from individual Enneagram points which are important in this second allocation of colours.

- From *Enneagram point 1*, in the red area, we look towards the primal polarity of the colours yellow (Enneagram point 7) and blue (Enneagram point 4).
- From *Enneagram point 2*, in the violet area, we look towards the complementary pair blue (point 4) and orange (point 8).
- From *Enneagram point 7*, the yellow, we also look towards a complementary pair: green (point 5) and red (point 1).

Figure 30 *The colours in the Enneagram (2)*

- There is, however, no perspective which unites the two complementaries yellow and violet.

The points of the triangle lead from the secondary colours to the three primary colours, or, as Rudolf Steiner puts it, from the surface colours to the lustrous colours. From Enneagram point 3, blue holds sway as the dark 'lustre' of the soul and leads us into the world of the unconscious and the feelings. From Enneagram point 6, yellow holds sway as the bright 'lustre of the spirit', leading us towards the clear world of consciousness and intellect. And at Enneagram point 9 (or 0), red holds sway as the living and colourful 'lustre of life', leading us into the material world of the body.

The primary or lustrous colours are thus to be found at Enneagram points 1, 4 and 7, while the secondary or surface colours are assigned to points 2, 5 and 8. This accords with Bennett's view that the two sets of Enneagram points – 1/4/7 and 2/5/8 – are structurally similar.[7] One could also say that

Enneagram point 1 unites all primary colours with each other and Enneagram point 8 unites all secondary colours.

At Enneagram point 7 we reach the highest stage of consciousness, where the pure yellow shines. At Enneagram point 8, in the orange sphere, this consciousness intensifies to the warmth of sympathy. Once we have reached our goal, we stand radiating warmth and light at the warm pole of the spectrum.

The light-colours

Let us once more briefly look at the way Goethe explains the light-colours, in his colour theory based on precise observation of the phenomena:

- The warm light-colours arise when cloudiness comes in front of a light source
- The cold light-colours arise when side-lit cloudiness comes in front of the darkness

Related to the Enneagram colours, this means: in the first allocation (*Figure 29*), we look from Enneagram points 1–3 towards darkness; we have not yet developed consciousness (light). From Enneagram point 6 we look towards the light: consciousness is born in us.

On the right side of the Enneagram, then, (points 1, 2, 3) we unite two wholly parallel processes. Only the perspective and angles are different: first we look towards the darkness (right Enneagram side); then towards the light (left Enneagram side). In our second allocation (*Figure 30*) we look from Enneagram points 2–4 in the direction of darkness; and from point 6 the light is born within us. It is important to recognize that both ways of assigning the colours to the Enneagram are of significance.

In his theory of the WHEEL,[8] Arnold Graf Keyserling offers a third possible colour order for the Enneagram, based on the prismatic refraction of colours; but I'm afraid that I find it difficult to comprehend.

The Jesuits also give a particular allocation of colours to the Enneagram; in my opinion, though, it does not accord at all with the nature of colours and the laws underlying them. It also has no similarity with the WHEEL theory. The Jesuits' ordering is as follows:

Point 1: Silver
Point 2: Red
Point 3: Yellow
Point 4: Mauve
Point 5: Cobalt blue
Point 6: Beige
Point 7: Green
Point 8: Black and white
Point 9: Gold

The very fact that we have here a combination of rainbow and non-rainbow colours, makes it hard to see a purposeful order in this system. This may have something to do with the fact that the colours themselves are not of primary interest here, but are simply being used to clarify the Jesuits' definition of the nine personality types.

Whichever of the two systematic allocations of the sixfold colour circle to the Enneagram I choose, they clearly demonstrate the salient laws and phenomena of the colours themselves. Since the rhythm of colours in the sixfold colour circle embodies an inwardly ordered, ensouled process, the Enneagram can be usefully applied to it. Both the Enneagram and the colour circle represent a system of archetypal images reflecting cosmic order and harmony. The colours, like people and their actions, as well as the cosmos itself and its planets, suns and solar systems, are all part of this order; and this is expressed clearly in both the Enneagram and the colour circle. Thus we can learn more about the Enneagram through the laws of colour; and vice versa, deepen our understanding of colour laws through the Enneagram.

Notes

1   Goethe, Johann Wolfgang von: *Faust 11*, verse 4727, Oxford University Press, 1994

2   Cf for a further examination of the colour symbolism of the primary colours: Vollmar, Klausbernd, *Farben – ihre natürliche Heilkraft*.

3   In the summer of 1920 Ouspensky helped Gurdjieff to prepare a revised version of this ballet, which was published after his death. Gurdjieff, G I, *The Struggle of the Magicians*. Many of the elements of this ballet found their way into the 'movement's' work. The costume colours for this ballet consisted of black dancers in opposition to white.

4   Goethe, Johann Wolfgang von, *Farbenlehre. Mit Einleitung und Kommentaren von Rudolf Steiner*. Also: Goethe (and E Merry): *Approach to Colour, Society of Metaphysicians*, 1988. And: Goethe, *Goethe's Theory of Colours*, Gordon Price, US, 1974.

5   The complementary colours are those which, in combination with each other, make a greyish mixture (or white, in the case of mixing light). They are always opposite to each other in the colour circle, at an angle of 180°.

6   Cf for more detailed examination of the colour symbolism of red: Vollmar, Klausbernd, *Das Geheimnis der Farbe Rot. Einladung zum Spiel mit dem Feuer. Ein Lese- und Übungsbuch zur Symbolik und Psychologie einer starken Farbe*.

7   Bennett, J G, *The Enneagram*.

8   Cf for more details on this: Neue Wiener Schule, *Im Jahr des Uranus;* and Keyserling, Arnold Graf, *Durch Sinnlichkeit zum Sinn*.

CHAPTER 6

The Cosmic Aspects

When we study man, we study the cosmos; when we study the cosmos we study man.

G I Gurdjieff

Before we can assign the individual planets to the Enneagram points, we must consider a few fundamental things. These are examined in Gurdjieff's chief work, *Beelzebub's Tales To His Grandson*, in a way that is sometimes very obscure, yet also humorous. As Gurdjieff said himself, this book should be read with the heart. I also think that it can be best understood by simultaneously practising self-remembering (as I described in Chapter 1 of this book). Reading it like this, the text is both funny and gripping. If we read it 'asleep', that is with poor attention, it immediately becomes boring and incomprehensible.

Beelzebub's Tales To His Grandson should be seen as a psychological system that tries to formulate a deep wisdom about the structure of the human being by looking at cosmic processes. The main protagonist Beelzebub can be regarded as the ideal of the conscious person. The archangels, such as Sakaki, who I will come back to later, symbolize the ideal power of intelligence; and a human is a being ruled not by consciousness (sun) but by the unconscious (moon).

The following sketches of a cosmology correspond to my own personal understanding of this highly esoteric work. There is certainly room for many differing interpretations of Gurdjieff's text. My particular approach reproduces Gurdjieff's cosmology in a way that is illuminating and uncontradictory, and which also has close connections with the Enneagram. It is worth remembering that when you study the cosmos and the Enneagram you are always also studying yourself.

Up to this point we have viewed the Enneagram as a helpful model for developing self-knowledge, for analysing economic processes, for creating a typology of character and for understanding the dynamics of colour. All these aspects of the Enneagram relate to the microcosmic level, to the human scale. The transition to the macrocosmic dimension of the Enneagram is embodied in the colours, which derive from light and so ultimately from the sun. Now let us begin to look at the Enneagram as a cosmic diagram.

Underlying the Enneagram teaching is a philosophical world-view that subscribes, like the philosophies of the Middle Ages and the Baroque period, to an approach based on the parallelism between microcosmos and macrocosmos. This approach can be traced back to the Tabula Smaragdina[1] of Hermes Trismegistos (about 200 BC), which says:[']

> That which is below is equal to that which is above: And that which is above is equal to that which is below, so as to fulfill the miraculous works of a single thing.

The Enneagram, as cosmic diagram, shows the manifold ways in which the laws of the cosmos influence the earth. The solar system, consisting of nine planets and the sun, can be depicted perfectly by means of the Enneagram, to show how microcosm and macrocosm follow a harmonious sequence and structure.

When my teacher first heard that I was writing this book about the Enneagram, he advised me to give particular attention to the cosmic aspects. In his opinion, these were the very essence of the Enneagram. I had personally found difficulty in penetrating this whole realm and thought that this was just another example of those notorious Gurdjieff tasks, which require people to get to grips with what they find most difficult. But as I pursued these studies, I began to realize that there was more to my teacher's advice than just overcoming my own difficulties and

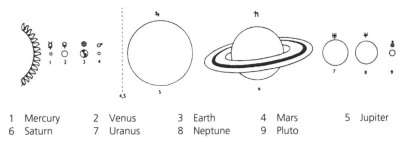

1 Mercury   2 Venus   3 Earth   4 Mars   5 Jupiter
6 Saturn   7 Uranus   8 Neptune 9 Pluto

Figure 31   *The planets of our solar system*

barriers. I now know that we can only understand the full dynamic of the Enneagram by penetrating the underlying cosmology of Gurdjieff. If we exclude this – on first sight rather theoretical and seemingly speculative – approach, our view and application of the Enneagram soon tends to become rigid; it turns into a dead symbol rather than a living dynamic.

Many teachers of the Fourth Way present the Enneagram as a model of Creation. They use it to show not only how our cosmos was formed, right down to subatomic particles, but also how the laws underlying the creation of the world are still at work in all sorts of ways. The Enneagram can reveal to us the ordering and the dynamic principle of Creation. I would now like to examine such laws.

The universe as living being

The parallelism between human being and cosmos allows us either to accentuate the cosmic dimension of the human being or the human dimension of the cosmos.

We have already touched on the cosmic dimension of the human being when describing the human energy centres, which are assigned to the inner heptagon of the Enneagram. In astrological terms we can see the following correspondences:

■ Root chakra (Muladhara): the Cancer/Capricorn axis

- Sex chakra (Svadhishthana): the Taurus/Scorpio axis
- Solar plexus chakra (Manipura): the Aries/Libra axis
- Heart chakra (Anahata): the Leo/Aquarius axis
- Throat chakra (Vishuddha): the Virgo/Pisces axis
- Crown chakra (Sahasrara): I would assign to the Sun, as symbol of the highest level of consciousness.[2]

The fact that the human body reflects cosmic processes is shown by Gurdjieff in the expression he uses for it in *Beelzebub's Tales*: 'planetary body'.

The human dimension of the cosmos has come to the fore in recent years, particularly through the Gaia hypothesis of the British scientist James Lovelock, which underpins the discipline called geophysiology. This views our planet in terms of nerves, blood vessels and muscular systems. Such an approach, though, is relevant not only to our earth, but also to the whole cosmos. Since the *Cabbala* and the early Christian work *De Principiis* by the gnostic philosopher Origenes (185–253/4), the universe has been seen as a giant organism whose soul is God. Based on this idea, the esoteric-gnostic tradition has, right up until our own times, taken the point of view that as human beings who are a small part of the whole, we see the body of the universe from within.

Just as the Enneagram can reflect all dynamic aspects of the human being, it can also descibe all the motions of the 'cosmic being'. To understand this we must now briefly examine how the cosmos came into existence at Creation.

The Creation and time

According to the schools of the Fourth Way, the Creation came about through a self-sacrifice of God. That is a view shared by traditional, orthodox Christianity. God as unmanifested or potential power becomes manifest or active energy, in the process of which he loses his unbounded freedom from all conditions and restraints. The creative power submits itself through this act of creation to the Law of Three; and is thus seen in Christian symbolism as the eye of God contained within the triangle – also, in Enneagram terms, finding its expression in the divine, equilateral triangle.

So the creative power, through the creative act, submits itself to the three laws of space, time and an intermediary harmonizing force. These three dimensions provide us with the fundamental life principles we know as passive (space), active (time) and neutral (the third or uniting force).

In the Enneagram, the three points of the triangle (points 3, 6, 9) form the three sections in which all earthly processes run their course.

- At *Enneagram point 3* we find the parasympathetic structure of the cosmic being, which directs its automatic functions.
- At *Enneagram point 6* is the sympathetic structure of this living cosmic being, which directs its unconscious functions.
- At *Enneagram point 9* is the cerebro-spinal function of the cosmos, which gives expression to its consciousness.

In other words, the automatic processes (point 3) occur in space; the unconscious processes (point 6) in time; and the harmonizing third function (point 9) makes sure that our cosmos is sustained and not destroyed by time and spatial processes. Just as Chronos/Saturn devours his children, time destroys all that has been made unless this process is hindered. In Assyrian and Babylonian mythology Saturn was known as the 'death-bringer'. The ancient Greeks, and even folk traditions which still survive, call Saturn/Chronos the 'Life-swallower'.

In order to prevent time from destroying the whole cosmos, the Law of Seven must also enter the Creation, alongside the uniting force.

This Law of Seven represents a particular parameter that can neutralize time's destructive influence. While the Law of Three is a natural consequence of the act of Creation, we recognize in the Law of Seven an artificially introduced condition. If this Law of Seven was not present, the three shock points of the

Enneagram could never keep a motion or process on its tracks, for it would die, as it were, from the effects of time.

This is how Gurdjieff, in *Beelzebub's Tales*, expresses the cosmic preconditions which once led to the forming of our universe. These are also the laws which underly the Enneagram as cosmic symbol. Gurdjieff dealt at great length and with great precision with the Law of Three, but did not, it seems to me, go into much detail on the Law of Seven.

Applied to the Enneagram, the Law of Seven (which corresponds to the octave in music) requires that a process run its whole course from point 1 to point 7 if it is to attain its aim. At Enneagram point 7 the goal is reached. Points 8 and 9 take us beyond our goal, thus representing its intensification and perfection to the point of embarking on a new octave.

To reach the goal in this way, we need the two shock points 3 and 6 – just as, in the scale, we find a half-tone step after the third and before the last note.

Having passed through the two shock points and arrived at the 7th Enneagram point, a cycle is completed. Since time is divided into various different cycles and periods, the schools of the Fourth Way speak of a 'curving of time'. This means that time is not to be thought of as a straightforward linear movement, but as a cyclical process: after seven stages a goal is reached; two further steps form the transition to a new cycle, which begins at Enneagram point 9 with renewed energy. Something dies so that something new can be born: one cycle takes over from another; and this repeats endlessly to the end of time.

Gurdjieff assumed that this curving of time was expressly intended by the Creator to prevent his Creation coming to an untimely end.

The Ray of Creation

In terms of physics, the Law of Three expresses the conditions pertaining in closed systems, in which no energy is lost, nor any new energy brought into play. The Law of Seven on the other hand corresponds to the Law of Reversibility, which says that in every exchange of energy, energy is lost until finally a stable condition of balance is reached. In modern physics these two laws are the first and second laws of thermodynamics. For Gurdjieff, though, the Law of Seven represents the law of motion of the living being of the cosmos. This law of motion is clearly expressed in the movements and holy dances which he based on the Enneagram sequences.

Before we address the actual position of the planets in the Enneagram, we must first briefly take a closer look at the place occupied by the planets, sun and moon in the order of Creation.

The whole of Creation is divided by the schools of the Fourth Way into seven sections.

- The first section represents unity, the Absolute, or, if you like, God.
- The second section contains all worlds that there are.
- In the third section we enter the realm of our own cosmos, the system of the Milky Way.
- In the fourth section we arrive at the sun.
- The fifth section contains the planets of our solar system.
- The sixth section contains our earth.
- The seventh section houses the moon.

This order of Creation is called the Sevenfold Ray of Creation (or, for short, the Ray of Creation). This can be seen as an image of different states of consciousness, stretching from the highest imaginable (the Absolute) to the unconscious (the moon).

In assigning the planets to the Enneagram we will be concerned, in the rest of this chapter, with the last four sections of the Ray of Creation: 4, 5, 6 and 7.

The Ray of Creation, descending from the Absolute unity down to the moon, represents a loss of freedom and power. The deeper we progress down this ladder, the more laws we are subject to.

- The Absolute unity is only subject to its own law, symbolized by the mid point of the circle within the Enneagram.
- All worlds are subject to the Law of Three, represented by the equilateral triangle in the Enneagram.
- Our Milky Way system is subject to the Law of Six, which corresponds to the hexagram in the Enneagram.
- Our sun is subject to 12, our planets to 24, our earth to 48 and the moon to 96 laws.

These precise figures themselves don't seem to me as important as the fact that every step of descent into lower worlds brings about an increased subjection to laws and a loss of freedom, right down to us earth-dwellers, who seem very bogged down and hemmed in!

The Sevenfold Ray of Creation also assigns an important role to the Enneagram shock points. World 6, our earth, is determined by its finite nature, while World 3, the Milky Way system, is still determined by infinity.

The structure of the Sevenfold Ray of Creation is not only subscribed to by the schools of the Fourth Way. The English Rosicrucian Robert Fludd (Robertus de Fluctibus, 1574–1634),

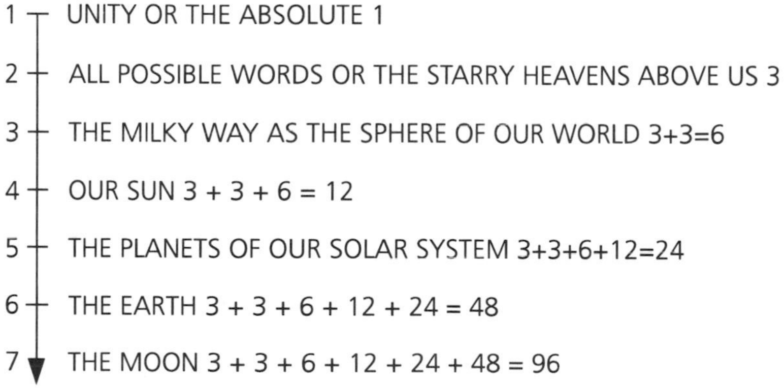

1 — UNITY OR THE ABSOLUTE 1

2 — ALL POSSIBLE WORDS OR THE STARRY HEAVENS ABOVE US 3

3 — THE MILKY WAY AS THE SPHERE OF OUR WORLD 3+3=6

4 — OUR SUN 3 + 3 + 6 = 12

5 — THE PLANETS OF OUR SOLAR SYSTEM 3+3+6+12=24

6 — THE EARTH 3 + 3 + 6 + 12 + 24 = 48

7 — THE MOON 3 + 3 + 6 + 12 + 24 + 48 = 96

Figure 32   *The Ray of Creation*

who as an alchemist was close to the ideas of Cabbalistic cosmology, posited a comparable, mathematically expressed harmony of the universe. In this harmony our sun also occupied the central place, precisely in the middle between the creative power of unity and the earth and moon.

This is just one of the many parallels between alchemical thinking and the schools of the Fourth Way. Both traditions love making use of mathematics and diagrams for the representation of microcosmic and macrocosmic processes. This approach resurfaces quite unexpectedly in German Romanticism when Novalis (the poet Friedrich Leopold Freiherr von Hardenberg, 1772–1801) coins the phrase: 'God is mathematics'.

We can distinguish three realms within the Ray of Creation (sun/planets/earth-moon) which once more reflect the Law of Three.[3] The sun gives life-energy, the planets provide outer form, and the earth offers up the material to be formed.

Assigning the planets

Gurdjieff believed that astrology was relevant to a person's type or inner being, not so much to the personality she developed. This fact is an important precondition for understanding the allocation of the planets to the Enneagram.

There are various ways in which – according to one's interest and preference – the planets can be assigned to Enneagram points. I personally work with a system that assumes the sun to be the focal point of the Enneagram circle, and positions the planets at points 1 to 9 according to the astronomical sequence of their orbits. This arrangement begins with the planet closest to the sun, Mercury, at point 1 and proceeds to the outermost planet, Pluto, at point 9.

I took my inspiration for this correspondence from the American astrologer Patrizia Norelli-Bachelet. I believe her largely forgotten *Astrology For Future Times*[4] to be a very thorough astronomical/astrological study of the Enneagram, which is unfortunately very hard-going to read.

In contrast, Rodney Collin's also very astronomically orientated study is easy to read. Collin's assigning of the planets to the Enneagram is based on the Path of Light (the degree of refelection of the planets): this is a very beautiful idea, but I do not think it leads to a satisfactory model of correspondence with the Enneagram. But this is not by any means the main thrust of Collin's very thoughtful work. He is more concerned, like all teachers of the Fourth Way, to find ways and means of awakening the human being.

Collin's study came out at the end of the sixties and Norelli-Bachelet's in the early seventies. It is astonishing that since then (with the exception of Arnold Graf Keyserling's WHEEL system) no further investigation of Enneagram astrology has been published; all the more so since the two other works have been out of print for years.

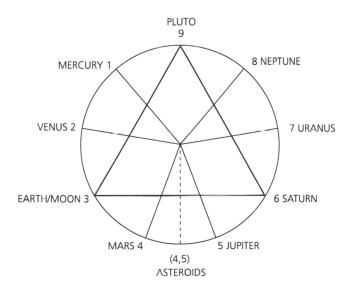

Figure 33 *Norelli-Bachelet's assigning of planets to the Enneagram*

My suggested model is neither identical with that of Norelli-Bachelet – it is actually a mirror image of it – nor with that of Rodney Collin, from whom I differ radically at points 3, 6 and 9.

As *Figure 34* shows, the planets are allocated to the individual points from a heliocentric point of view. That means that they are seen in a way that accords with the real astronomical relationships of our solar system. The sun forms the focal point of this system; then come the planets ordered according to the distance of their orbit from the sun. So we obtain the sequence: Mercury, Venus, moon and earth – as planets belonging together (which I will explain in more detail shortly); then Mars, Jupiter, Saturn, Uranus, Neptune and the outermost planet Pluto. At the three points of the triangle (3, 6, 9) are to be found the three most significant planets of the solar system.

At Enneagram point 3 stands the earth with its satellite the moon, as the planet on which human life has reincarnated as

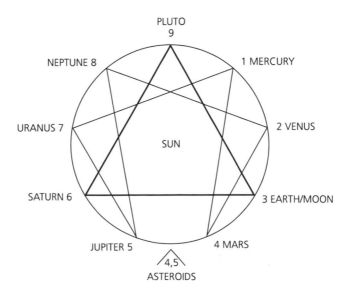

Figure 34   *The planets in the Enneagram*

the highest level of all life. At point 6 lies Saturn, the Guardian of the Threshold, as the last planet we can still distinguish from earth with the naked eye. The moon at point 3 and Saturn at point 6 are related to each other inasmuch as the moon takes 29 days to pass through all the signs of the zodiac, while Saturn takes 29 years.[5]

From Enneagram point 1 to point 6 we find the personal planets: classical astrology views all the planets this side of Saturn as personal, and those beyond – the 'trans-Saturn' planets – as transpersonal, because these have very long periods of orbit and therefore rule generations and epochs. The classical planets this side of Saturn, with their faster orbits, influence the life of individuals.[6] At Enneagram point 9 stands Pluto, the most distant planet of our solar system, whose influence on the human being is considered by classical astrology to be of the utmost subtlety. Therefore I assign the earth/moon, Saturn, and Pluto to the three shock points of the Enneagram.

To illustrate the practical side of this planetary law of the Three, I would like to quote a passage from my diary.

Normally when I have to make a decision I'm completely dependent on my associations with the particular situation. These are generally fairly haphazard and keep me locked in to my mechanistic behaviour patterns, so that I'm largely dependent on a mixture of dualistic thinking and feeling. So I stay caught up in my narrow limitations, and tied to my own experiences.

But last week I was able to realize that it's possible to overcome these limitations in situations where decisions are called for. After going over all the pros and cons about separating from X, I sat down and tried to remember myself in a fully relaxed state. After searching for calm for some while, I felt the streaming of forces within my body; then I asked an unknown power to give me insight. In a way I offered myself to that third force, allowing it to work in and through me. Today when I woke up my decision was suddenly quite clear.

The so-called invisible binding force worked in me and helped me to make a decision that went beyond the confines of my limited, dualistic thinking. At the same time I realized that I cannot force or compel this power to come to my aid. I can only open myself to it. This is what folk wisdom expresses in the phrase: 'Let's sleep on it'.

The third force introduces a new dimension into ways of looking at a decision; it helps us grow beyond our automatic reactions. It also provides us with the emotional certainty we need to follow through a decision without being sidetracked. The cosmic Law of Three works through us and allows us to live in unity with cosmic rhythms. 'All good things come in threes' is a saying which now makes more sense to me.

If we extend this insight to the three planets at the three shock points of the Enneagram, then earth and moon correspond to our emotions and actual circumstances, upon which we often feel passively dependent. Those are the 'pros', the passive aspects of a decision which would prefer to keep things as they have always been. The 'cons' correspond to Saturn which compels us to face the truth and would like to tempt us over the threshold into new and other realms. The invisible, subtle binding force, the 'still, quiet voice' to which we open ourselves in peaceful self-remembering, is symbolized by Pluto. It represents the real, transformative force without which every decision remains unsatisfactory. Pluto, as a transpersonal planet, helps us grow beyond the narrow limitations of our ego into a wider, cosmic context.

An inner decision reflects cosmic processes. We function like the great cosmic being outside us – or, as holography says: 'The structure of every part of a whole is formed in much the same way as the whole itself.'

In my Enneagram planet allocation, we can also see that in the Enneagram's 'problem-zone' – at a point exactly midway between points 4 and 5, which we called 'The Hero's Night Sea Voyage' – the asteroid belt is to be found. This is not an Enneagram point as such, but it plays an important role as a difficult, invisible boundary. Like the actual asteroid belt, it does not have a clearly defined centre or space.

The asteroid belt is a cosmic reflection of our negative moods – which are often hard to grasp or define. We are all familiar with doubts, fears and so on. These psychic structures are not clearly formed and crystallized (they have not yet, in other words, become fixed – thank goodness!). We can't really get to grips with them but instead suffer passively from the limitations they impose on us. Psychotherapy calls them 'free-floating anxieties'.

Enneagram point 1: Mercury

The small planet Mercury is nearest to the sun. In the 'healing' direction of the Enneagram, Mercury is connected with Uranus (point 7), which is thought of as its 'octave'.

Mercury represents the starting point of our 'Enneagram of the planets'; and we can recall that in mythology Mercury is actually not a god but a messenger of the gods. We only enter the realm of the gods and goddesses from Enneagram point 2 onwards.

This archetype – who offers protection to all traders and business men – corresponds perfectly to the Enneagram type 1, the 'Entrepreneur'. Mercury is closely connected with the realm of matter, and is therefore in the right place at the beginning of the first third of the Enneagram, where we are getting to grips with everything of a material nature. The association of Mercury with matter can be traced back to very ancient times. In ancient Egypt, Mercury (Thoth) was a symbol for using matter. In our Western culture, Mercury was thought of as the god of alchemy, the art of transforming matter. We are concerned here, ultimately, with the transformation of our own body. Gurdjieff was convinced that any progress in consciousness is always also expressed in the physical body. Through spiritual development even the inner cell structure is affected and changed.

In the first third of the Enneagram we find the highest degree of movement and speed of reaction. Mercury fits perfectly here: as well as the planet having the fastest orbit round the sun, Mercury is also known in mythology as the fastest of all travellers.

But we rarely have a chance to observe its quick motion, for of all the visible planets it appears least often. In Europe, it can only be seen for about 15 to 18 hours a year.

Enneagram point 2: Venus

Enneagram point 2 is connected with Enneagram point 8, Neptune, which represents its octave.

Venus is also connected with Mars at Enneagram point 4. Venus and Mars belong together mythologically as lovers. Astrologically, Mars and Venus are inseparable because they rule the two complementary signs Libra and Aries. This means that as rulers of their respective signs they lie on a horoscope axis.

Like Mercury, Venus stays relatively close to the sun, and is archetypally related to the moon. Both Venus and the moon symbolize the emotional side of human beings.[7] Venus is to be found at Enneagram point 2, the transition place towards the moon realm.

Venus and Mercury, at the two first Enneagram points distinguish themselves from all other planets of our solar system by the fact that they both alternate periodically between being morning and evening stars. Venus symbolizes – in depth-psychology terms – the forming, shaping power of the human being; it is therefore at home with the Enneagram type 2, the 'Shaper'.

Enneagram point 3: earth and moon

For Gurdjieff, our planet earth – which he liked to call 'purgatory' – represents the heart of the cosmos, in which all 'results' (of all existing forms in the cosmos) concentrate.

As we saw in the character typology of the Enneagram (Chapter 4), at point 3 – the first (mechanical) shock point – feeling enters the system as a new quality. Feeling or psyche is inseparably connected with the moon; according to astrology and also the schools of the Fourth Way, it influences our moods. This emotional dependency on the moon has always been a factor in folk tradition and medicine.

According to Gurdjieff, earth and moon are an indivisible unity; he believed that the moon nourishes itself from human emotions. This may be an off-putting sort of concept – who wants to believe we are exploited by the moon? Whenever this is mentioned in Gurdjieff groups there is a great deal of resistance to the idea.

In *Beelzebub's Tales*, Gurdjieff describes how, in very ancient times, a great wandering planet, named Kondoor, collided with the earth. This occurred as a result of the miscalculations of a certain holy being. Kondoor hit the still uninhabited earth with such force that two large parts were blown out of it and hurled into a geocentric orbit. One of these parts was the moon, the other Gurdjieff calls Anulios.

Now good advice was sorely needed, for the moon which had come about as a result of this catastrophe caused chaos in the harmony of the solar system. So the cosmic engineer and archangel Sakaki was given the task of re-establishing rightful order as quickly as possible. Sakaki's master-stroke was to stabilize the moon through the holy vibration which Gurdjieff calls 'Askokin'. This is emitted at the death of living organisms. Sakaki therefore had to create the various living organisms on earth, so that the vibrations emitted at their death could continue to stabilize the moon. From these living organisms, humanity eventually evolved.

But Sakaki was worried that as their consciousness developed, human beings would collectively object to this moon-exploitation. If they should recognize that all their suffering and striving only served to keep the moon stable, things would soon start to turn sour. Sakaki even envisaged the possibility of a mass suicide by humanity if this fact became widely known. That had to be prevented at all costs. So he implanted an organ into the human race which Gurdjieff calls 'Kundabuffer', reminiscent of the Indian kundalini. This Kundabuffer organ prevents people having any clear insight into their situation. And so the sleep of humanity began.

Thus human beings served the moon in a blind and unconscious way. The moon, like a hungry baby, sucked the life of the earth not from malice or aggression, but from the cosmic necessity of evolving. Once the moon at last became somewhat more stable, Sakaki immediately removed the Kundabuffer organ. But without much effect: people had meanwhile become as dependent on the moon as the moon had been on them. With or without Kundabuffer, human behaviour patterns remained the same. To become conscious once more, the 'work' is needed – without it we continue to live in slavish dependency on the moon.

So here we have Gurdjieff's descriptions. I don't want to adopt a post-modernist attitude towards them and immediately equate the Gurdjieffian moon with the unconscious or with Freud's Id. For the time being I prefer to stay in the realms of astronomy and cosmology.

Just as in Gurdjieff's thinking, both science and mythology have also seen the moon as a child of the earth. In the 19th century, there was a scientific theory which held that the moon was originally a part of the earth, and had been split off from it in a cosmic catastrophe. This idea also informs the Greek myth which says that the Titan Theia gave birth to the moon-goddess Selene.

At any rate, the moon is certainly a satellite, dependent on the earth. It is an unusual satellite, though, because it has such a large mass – equal to about an eightieth part of the earth. The sun, on the other hand, upon which all planets of our solar system are dependent, has a mass 800 times greater than the mass of all the planets put together. Also, in comparison to the orbits of other planets, the moon's orbit round the earth is very close indeed. To put it in human terms, one could say that the earth is very burdened by the moon. The astrologer Rodney Collin says that our earth is 'the most heavily burdened planet of the solar system.'

This great mass of the moon has a counter weight effect on the earth's motion. The moon is like the pendulum weight of the earth. Without this counter weight, astrophysicists think that the earth would no longer remain in its orbit, but would vanish off into the depths of the cosmos.

It is generally known that the moon influences the tides; but this influence is not confined to the waters of the ocean alone – all fluids are affected. The human being, consisting of some 72 per cent water, is also subject to the moon's attraction, which prevents us being laid out flat on the earth's surface like a puddle. Through the moon's influence we can overcome the pull of gravity to the extent of standing upright and walking.

When I was living in Findhorn, I acted as secretary for a while to an old lady, a Scottish medium who 'received' messages which had some connection with the Enneagram. During the weeks that I took care of her paperwork, I was never quite sure whether she was off her head or a genius. She asserted that the Enneagram represented an evolutionary model of human history. She placed Lemuria at Enneagram point 1, and said that it had been mankind's task to evolve from Lemuria to Atlantis (Enneagram point 2). This process of evolution was connected with assuming an upright posture. In Lemuria, the earth's gravity had a stronger effect on people than the moon's pull, so that human beings of that time had to go on all fours. By the period of Atlantis, people had learnt to make use of the moon's attraction so as to stand upright.

It still seems remarkable to me that this old lady had never read Gurdjieff, yet had similar ideas about the moon's role. This suggests the deep archetypal source of such imaginings about the moon's magnetism.

So the moon enables the bodily fluids to rise when the human being is in an upright position (walking, sitting or standing).[8] The pumping action of the heart increases this dynamic, but the lymph depends almost wholly on it, as well as on osmosis – the exchange between different concentrations of a solution – and on physical movement.

My medium also believed that all movements of the human body are more or less dependent on the moon. This corresponds with Rodney Collin's telling statement, that 'the moon calls forth movements in us whether we like it or not'.[9] In other words, every conscious movement, but more particularly every unconscious one – all our habits and ticks – are under the moon's sway. In the schools of the Fourth Way to which Rodney Collin belongs, the development of consciousness is seen as a process of liberation from the moon's influence.

So the moon is the great magnet of nature, keeping all living beings upright and alive. Its power of attraction on the earth is three times stronger than that of all other planets put together.

Now let us look at the moon itself. In contrast with the earth, there is absolutely no movement upon its surface. Nothing happens there, nothing changes. There is no wind, no seasons, no rainfall, let alone any growth. At most there might occasionally be a dust cloud if a meteor hits it!

The moon does not turn around its own axis; it does not, in other words, possess any power to separate different materials or masses from each other. A satellite with its own rotation and centrifugal force, makes itself to some degree independent from its 'parent' planet. The centrifugal forces give rise to selection mechanisms and thus provide a first stimulus for independent movement of the satellite, but for this to happen, the 'child' must be at some distance from the 'parent' – a distance far greater than the moon has yet achieved. The moon would have to be twice as far from the earth to develop its own rotation. The moon is completely dependent on the earth, like a child who has not yet attained emancipation.

To free itself from the earth, the moon urgently needs to develop its own motion. According to the schools of the Fourth Way, it tries to acquire this motion through sucking or magnetic effects. It draws the energies of organic life away from the earth so that it can grow. The followers of the schools of the Fourth Way explain the cause of wars in this astonishingly apolitical way: the moon has a great hunger and so draws life away from the earth. This is comparable to the embryo in the womb being nourished by the mother's bloodstream, or the suckling movements of the infant at its mother's breast.

So moon and earth are intimately connected, like mother and child. The moon draws nourishment from the earth in order to become an independent planet and to escape from its parent's sphere of influence. This is why earth and moon stand together at Enneagram point 3. This mechanical shock point is called forth by the moon, since it is so closely connected with the human being's automatic, unconscious movements. It is therefore easy to see why the moon is on the lowest level of the Sevenfold Ray: it is the most childlike of all planetary bodies.

After looking at the moon in this cosmic light, we can now feel fully justified in equating it with our unconscious. Emma Jung writes that the unconscious 'opposes every process of becoming aware, or threatens to darken or extinguish the awareness that has been attained'. She also says that the unconscious 'emits a continual force of attraction, that can be compared with the effect of gravity'.[10] To oppose this attraction requires almost superhuman power. Gurdjieff's statements about the moon and Emma Jung's descriptions of the unconscious are very similar, even at the level of the imagery and metaphor they both employ.

All that lives and is therefore subject to death, is inevitably drawn into the sphere of influence of the unconscious, where it is deprived of all possibility of change. C J Jung also believed that nothing much changes in the deep ground of the soul, at the level of the collective unconscious. Yet he thought that it does, very gradually, draw nourishment from experiences that have sunk down into people's individual unconscious, and so transforms itself over very great periods of time.

If an individual wants to fight against her unconscious processes in order to change herself, she has to do it by cunning. If this does not succeed, the unconscious draws her back into her old patterns of behaviour. The struggle against the sucking power of the unconscious, which was of particular interest to Jung's pupil Erich Neumann (1905–1960),[11] allows us to become more flexible.

The cosmic accident that split off the moon and Anulios from the earth, takes its course in each one of us. It is embodied in the influence of education and socialization, which leads us away from the holistic state of childhood, in which all three centres are united with one another, to the fragmented adult.

Moon and Anulios were split off – that means that our feeling, intellectual and motor centres are separated from one another with the result that we become split personalities. Such a personality is at the mercy of her unconscious, and far removed from the possibility of making clear decisions and so developing a directed will. The active intellectual centre no longer tries to connect with the passive feeling centre; and the neutral motor and instinctual centre lives cut off and forgotten in its own bubble. So the human being develops in one-sided ways; she feels torn apart when it comes to making decisions and is ultimately manipulated by all kinds of chance external factors.

Mercury, Venus and the moon, belonging to the first third of the Enneagram of planets, lie closer to the sun than the earth's orbit, and can be seen with the naked eye. At Enneagram points 4, 5 and 6, we find the planets Mars, Jupiter and Saturn: these, belonging to the second third of the Enneagram, are the planets whose orbits are further away from the sun than the earth, but can also still be seen with the naked eye.

Enneagram point 4: Mars

The mutual relationship between earth and moon stands at the first Enneagram shock point, where the world of the psyche and feelings enters in. In mythology, Mars is, among other things, a planet of aggression and so of negative feelings – which is what we have to struggle with at this stage of the process (point 4). Mars is the planet that shows the greatest variations both in distance from the earth, and therefore also in brightness.[12] These variations in brightness symbolize, at point 4, the struggle between light and dark in the human psyche. In addition, the rhythm of its motions and visibility is the most complex of all the planets.[13] This corresponds to the enormous complexity of human emotions.

The second third of the Enneagram of planets is formed by three planets: Mars (point 4), Jupiter (point 5) and Saturn (point 6). All planets of this section are characterized by the specific periodicity of their visibility. At the time of their conjunction with the sun they are invisible. At such times, they rise and set at the same time as the sun. After a few weeks of invisibility, they become visible before dawn in the eastern sky (heliactic rise). From that point on the particular planet rises earlier and earlier, and can be seen more and more clearly in the second half of the night. Eventually it can also be seen before midnight, until at last it becomes visible at sunset. At this time it possesses its greatest radiance and visibility. Mars, Jupiter or Saturn then shine throughout the night. In the following months the duration of their visibility continually decreases once more, until they can be seen only for a short while after sunset, and then finally become invisible again.

The rhythmic repetition of the same positions in the sky occurs for Saturn and Jupiter every year and for Mars every two years. The three planets of the second third of the Enneagram all have this motion in common.

Enneagram points 4/5: The asteroid belt

On New Year's Day 1801, the Italian astronomer G Piazzi discovered the first of the asteroids or planetoids, which he named Ceres. Nowadays we know of several thousand asteroids. The orbit of all of them passes between Mars and Jupiter.

> The asteroid belt, the 4/5 orbit, is the decisive turning point, where, as it were, the breaks are applied so as to powerfully impede the force vibrating out of the focal centre, and to return it, with the help of the movement deriving from the realm of subtle matter and energy, to its source.[14]

Beyond the asteroid belt, we find the four largest planets of our solar system: Jupiter (point 5), the largest planet after the sun, Saturn (point 6), the second largest planet, with its characteristic rings, and Uranus (point 7) and Neptune (point 8) which are almost the same size as each other. According to Norelli-Bachelet, the asteroid belt provides a connection between matter and spirit, which alone can save the earth from its decline and disintegration. Without this asteroid belt the solar system would continue to expand, and the subtle energies of the spirit (the trans-Saturn planets) would become more and more distant from the earth. Norelli-Bachelet speculates that the influence of the planets beyond the asteroid belt approaches the earth in something like a great curve, so that our planet can receive subtle spiritual energies from them. This curvature, which ultimately allows the furthest planets to enter into a close contact with us, is, according to Norelli-Bachelet, 'not to be understood with our concepts of space and time.'[15] It is, rather, a mysterious movement beyond the grasp of our consciousness.

I have to admit that my male intellect has the greatest difficulty in accepting such speculations. The asteroid belt, for me, represents that invisible boundary which Gurdjieff called 'Harnelahut': the difficult transition from Enneagram point 4 to point 5. This is a threshold of consciousness which separates the right side of the Enneagram from the left, and which can only be crossed through conscious suffering and striving. The fact that the asteroid belt does not have a condensed centre, perfectly echoes the psychological difficulties encountered at this stage. One is confronted by something that cannot be grasped. Such a force is described very beautifully in Henrik Ibsen's drama *Peer Gynt*, in which the invisible Great Curve hinders the hero Peer Gynt from pursuing a straight and direct path. At this stage of the Enneagram we learn that the direct path is not always passable, and that ultimately it may well not be the shortest route. The geometry of the psyche does not correspond to that of Euclid.

Enneagram point 5: Jupiter

At Enneagram point 5 stands the largest planet of our solar system. From here on they decrease in size. Jupiter lies midway between the sun and the orbit of Pluto. This corresponds exactly to its position at point 5. All the stars in its neighbourhood are outshone by Jupiter, which is symbolic of the point 5 scenario – in spite of all suffering, one can now see the context of one's life and the goal one is aiming for.

Once we have overcome the asteroid belt we are on the right path, which lies before us illuminated by Jupiter's radiance. Roman mythology called Jupiter the 'Father of Light'. According to the Roman poet and philosopher Titus Lucrezia (about 98–55 BC), Jupiter is the source and origin of light.

Enneagram point 6: Saturn

Saturn was discovered in 1610 by the Italian astronomer and mathematician Galileo Galilei (1564–1642).

Saturn is the last planet which can still be seen with the naked eye. It is very hard, though, to see it, and so it represents a transition towards invisibility, which is why this faint bluish planet is called the 'Guardian of the Threshold'. Its rings are unusual, composed of a complicated system of micro-planetoids.

As Chronos, Saturn is the god of time, responsible for all evolution and development. He is both the instigator and destroyer of the Creation. Like the Indian goddess Kali[16] and the god Shiva, Saturn is both destroyer and creator; a symbol of both death and rebirth.

In psychological terms, Saturn was thought to be an entity providing structure and order, and demanding responsible action. As such he belongs in the realm of the intellect or mind. Intellectual energy enters the Enneagram system as a new, conscious quality at the second shock point; just as feeling accompanied the moon at the first. With Saturn at point 6, we cross over the threshold to the finer and more subtle influences and vibrations of the trans-Saturn planets. Here begins the last third of the Enneagram.

The whole of Gurdjieff's teachings have something of a Saturn-like nature, which can initially be very off-putting for many seekers. My teacher once made a statement about our group which was characteristic of this kind of approach: 'We are not here', he said, 'to be friendly to one another, but to love each other. We don't want to draw nice, good-natured people into the group, but people whose lives, as they have been up to now, appear unbearable to them.' The continual emphasis in Gurdjieff groups on the 'work' and the effort needed, are indicative of this Saturn character.

The trans-Saturn planets

The planets Uranus, Neptune and Pluto begin a new octave in the system. This second octave represents a new level of the qualities previously encountered in Mercury, Venus and Mars.

These three planets of the second octave are invisible to us without magnification because, in contrast to the planets of the first octave, they do not reflect enough sunlight. It is interesting to discover that their long orbital paths through the zodiac relate to one another in a ratio of 1:2:3. Uranus takes about seven years, Neptune about fourteen and Pluto about twenty-one.

I can't resist mentioning a further interesting numerological fact. Uranus was discovered in 1781, at 25° in the star sign Gemini. These degrees give us a numerological 7 (2 + 5 = 7). Uranus is on the seventh orbit from the sun, at Enneagram point 7. Neptune was discovered in 1846, at 26° in the sign of Aquarius, which gives us a numerological 8 (2 + 6 = 8). Neptune is on the eighth heliocentric orbit and is assigned to Enneagram point 8. Pluto was discovered in 1930, at 18° in the sign of Cancer. This gives us 9 (1 + 8 = 9). Pluto is on the ninth heliocentric orbit and belongs to the ninth Enneagram point. Is this an astonishing coincidence of cosmic mathematics? But as Einstein said: 'God does not play dice'.

Enneagram point 7: Uranus

Uranus at Enneagram point 7 is the culmination of the first octave, which began with Mercury. The seeker has here reached her goal.

The love of Uranus for Gaia symbolizes the perfect relationship between heaven and earth. The creative and receptive principles unite with one another to form a new unity. But in Greek mythology this union was not blessed with joy for very long, for Uranus, from fear of losing his power, commits child murder. Gaia then incites her son Chronos/Saturn to rebel against his own father. This leads to the castration of Uranus, which is symbolic of the end of the primal act of creation.[17]

The first cycle of creation comes to an end with Uranus. One is now free either to continue to pursue one's task or to rest content with what has been achieved. At Enneagram point 7, the place of Uranus, we have to decide whether to carry on. According to the Italian astrologer Roberto Sicuteri, this planet is capable of dissolving the ego.[18] This is exactly the same as my previous statement that from point 7 onwards, serving others comes into its own. Norelli-Bachelet sees Uranus as the 'power to transform the spirit',[19] which is her term for overcoming the ego. But since Uranus is still at the very beginning of this process of development, he also possesses a mighty shadow that can tempt us to pursue our goals in an unscrupulous, egocentric, impulsive and aggressive way. Uranus as the planet of freedom that is here attained at Enneagram point 7, begs the question about how this freedom will actually be used.

This greenish-blue planet can only be seen with a telescope. It was discovered in 1781 by a German astronomer living in England, Sir Friedrich Wilhelm Herschel (1738–1822).

Enneagram Point 8: Neptune

In both astronomical and astrological terms, Uranus and Neptune are twins: both have a similar loop trajectory; and both cannot only awaken altruistic feelings but also demonstrate a strong shadow aspect that can lead to chaos.

Sixty-five years after Herschel's sighting of Uranus, Neptune was discovered. Neptune confronts us with a higher octave of Venus. Venus is harmony, perfection and emotion, which is expressed in its almost perfectly circular orbit.

From Enneagram point 8 we encounter the finer vibrations of feeling. Neptune continues the task, begun by Uranus, of freeing us from the ego; but we should not underestimate his powerful shadow that can spread illusion and cloud our perceptions. This can make a person at Enneagram point 8 believe she is serving higher aims, although it is really her ego that is being flattered.

While Uranus, as god of the sky, has a connection with the element of air, Neptune/Poseidon rules over the waters, which the alchemists associated with depth of feeling and sensibility. Through this intense connection with the emotions, a person at Enneagram point 8 can easily become a sympathetic mediator, helping a large group to run smoothly.

Enneagram point 9: Pluto

Pluto is the last planet of the last third of the Enneagram. It represents the octave of Mars, although it is not connected to Mars by the Enneagram's inner lines. Some astrologers say that Pluto at the top point of the Enneagram can be seen as a representative of the sun. Pluto symbolizes the nuclear energy that was set free for the first time in humanity's history at the same time that this last planet was discovered. This 'nuclear fire' can be compared to the sun. Pluto, also known and feared as Hades by the Greeks, stands for the tension between destruction and creation, and so is in some respects similar to Saturn.

In Greek mythology, Pluto was honoured as the god of wealth and abundance, of fruitfulness and fertility; yet this did not blind people to his huge shadow aspect – as Hades, god of the underworld, whose name they hardly dared mention. Like Saturn, Pluto in his Hades aspect represented a guardian of the threshold, in this case the threshold to the underworld.

Pluto/Hades creates connections to other undreamed-of worlds and dimensions; its orbit alone, which passes through the remote depths of the cosmos, far away from the sun, expresses this. Pluto at the ninth point of the Enneagram oversees the transition into a new dimension or level of a process.

Because of its position there, it can also be seen as the uniting power or force (atomic fusion!) without which no process can come to completion. Pluto, ruling over both fertility and destruction – and thus encompassing all of life – connects all aspects of life with each other. This is precisely what Freud meant by Eros and Thanatos: Eros as the urge to life and Thanatos as the death-urge are the two forces which determine all human experience. In Pluto, Eros and Thanatos are united.

All three trans-Saturn planets of the third triad are connected astrologically with a specific energy. Uranus corresponds to electricity, Neptune to fossil fuel (oil) and Pluto to atomic energy (Plutonium); of the three, clearly atomic energy is the most powerful. The medium and theosophist Alice A Bailey (A A B, 1880–1949) believed that Plutonic energy with its radioactive radiation would play an important part in the transformation of humanity.

The following table sums up the order of the planets in the Enneagram.

The Path of Light

Rodney Collin, an astrologer who closely follows the indications of Ouspensky and Gurdjieff, also tried to assign the planets of our solar system to the Enneagram. But in contrast to Norelli-Bachelet, his approach is based not on a heliocentric system of concentric planetary orbits, but on a classical view of the planets in their relationship to the earth. He starts from the assumption that scientific observation of the planets has to be rooted in a geocentric view, and that therefore the perspective from our own planet is the only objective one. His ordering of the planets therefore distinguishes between those which are visible and those which are invisible to the naked eye.

The asteroid belt, Neptune, Uranus and Pluto are invisible, while the moon, sun, Mercury, Venus, Mars, Jupiter and Saturn are visible. Collin posits a path of light between the seven visible planetary bodies, and it is upon this that his system is

The personal inner-orbit planets, visible with the naked eye

Enneagram point 1   Mercury, the fastest planet
Enneagram point 2   Venus
Enneagram point 3   Earth and moon

The outer-orbit planets, visible with the naked eye

Enneagram point 4   Mars, with the most complex orbital path
Enneagram point 5   Jupiter, the largest of the planets
Enneagram point 6   Saturn, with its rings

The transpersonal planets, invisible to the naked eye

Enneagram point 7   Uranus (octave of Mercury)
Enneagram point 8   Neptune (octave of Venus)
Enneagram point 9   Pluto (octave of Mars)

Also not visible to the naked eye, and not condensed to a centre

Point 4/5   The asteroid belt

---

based. The six planets and the moon all reflect the same sun-light, while the asteroid belt, Uranus, Neptune and Pluto are not involved in this reflection process.

The path of light has its source in the sun, which in this Enneagram is assigned to a position below the intersection point of the two hexagram lines inside the Enneagram, below Enneagram point 9. The moon (point 1) and Jupiter (point 7) are the two brightest poles of this Enneagram, and are therefore directly connected with each other. Saturn at Enneagram point 8 and Mercury at point 2 are the two darkest poles; they are also connected to each other by a hexagram line.

The inner Enneagram point of the sun is not only the point of most intense brightness in our solar system, but also the point of invisibility of every planet in conjunction with the sun. This view allows us to proceed through all the possible intensities of reflection of sunlight, passing from the point of invisibility towards Saturn at point 8 (dark), then past Mars (point 5) to the brightest planet on the left side of the Enneagram, Jupiter at point 7, and then continuing back to the sun once more.

On the right side of the Enneagram we start from dark Mercury at point 2, pass Venus (point 4) and reach the bright moon at point 1, in a fully parallel motion to the left side. On this path of light the planets also alternate in size:

Saturn (large, dark) – Mars (smaller) – Jupiter (larger, bright) – Mercury (small, dark) – Venus (larger) – moon (smaller, bright).

As we can see, there are several possible ways of assigning the planets to the Enneagram. The two shown here are not the only ones. It would also be possible to ascribe the hexagram points 1, 2, 4, 5, 7 and 8 to Mercury, Venus, earth/moon, Mars, Jupiter and Saturn, and the three shock points to the trans-Saturn planets Uranus, Neptune and Pluto. This would emphasize the fact that the planets of our solar system can be arranged in two

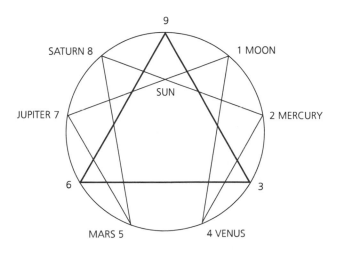

Figure 35   The Enneagram of planetary light

different octaves, which are distinguished from each other, among other things, by different qualities of visibility. But I do not think such an Enneagram would have much else to tell us.

Arnold Graf Keyserling, in his WHEEL system, orders the planets in the following way:

Enneagram point 1: Jupiter
Enneagram point 2: Venus
Enneagram point 3: Uranus
Enneagram point 4: Moon
Enneagram point 5: Mercury
Enneagram point 6: Neptune
Enneagram point 7: Mars
Enneagram point 8: Saturn
Enneagram point 9: Pluto

The three trans-Saturn planets are therefore on the Enneagram points of the divine triangle; but the allocation of the other planets seems to me subject to no recognizable logic.[20]

There are always several different ways of assigning elements to the Enneagram, but they are not always of much help or use. The art of working with the Enneagram consists of allowing the inner dynamic of a given process to unfold as many different aspects as possible. The Enneagram only helps us if we gain insights and information from it that we didn't previously possess.

The star signs in the Enneagram

Now that we have looked in detail at the planets, I would like to provide a possible way of assigning the star signs to the Enneagram.

In *Beelzebub's Tales* Gurdjieff makes it quite clear in several places that he thinks modern astrologers are a waste of time. He calls them 'Ultra-fantasists'. The ancient astrologers, in contrast, who according to him died out in Egyptian times, were useful because they could help people select partners who suited them. The most beneficial moment for conception could also be determined astrologically. Without wanting to go down the 'Ultra-fantasy' road, I would still like to show how the cosmic order of the zodiac can be integrated into the cosmic symbol of the Enneagram.

In the ordering depicted in *Figure 36*, the first thing to notice is that the three fire signs, Aries, Leo and Sagittarius, are assigned to the divine triangle. The three forms of divine fire rule this Enneagram: fire does not only warm, it also radiates the light of knowledge and has a transforming character.

Our journey through the zodiac begins at Enneagram point 9, which is at the same time Enneagram point 0. Here we find the cardinal energy of beginning (Aries energy) which then roots and solidifies itself with the fixed energy at Enneagram point 3 (Leo energy). But this movement neither comes to a halt nor rigidifies, for the mutable energy at point 6 (Sagittarius energy) gives it a new impetus.

The hexagram line from Enneagram point 1 to point 7 combines the fixed with the cardinal energy. The mutable earth energy of Virgo at point 4 is again connected with the fixed earth energy of Taurus at point 1. Similarly, the hexagram line from point 2 to point 8 connects the cardinal with the mutable water energy. This mutable water energy at point 8 is also connected with the fixed water energy at point 5.

So this Enneagram of the zodiac fully embodies the fire and water signs in the form of Yin and Yang. The three earth signs are likewise connected with one another. Standing at Enneagram point 1, we see all the earth signs. From point 8 we see all the water signs, and from point 9 all the fire signs. The signs enclosed by pairs of Enneagram points, rather than on them, are the three air signs: Gemini, Libra and Aquarius.

Passing through this Enneagram in its functional direction, the rhythm: water – fire – earth (feeling – passion/will – getting to grips with reality) is accentuated three times. The intellect is not specially emphasized in this Enneagram, since it is already so pronounced in our culture.

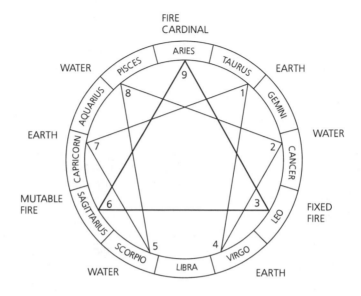

Figure 36   *The star signs in the Enneagram*

So we arrive at the following allocation of the zodiac signs.

Point 1	Taurus	earth	fixed
Point 2	Cancer	water	cardinal
Point 3	Leo	fire	fixed
Point 4	Virgo	earth	mutable
Point 5	Scorpio	water	fixed
Point 6	Sagittarius	fire	mutable
Point 7	Capricorn	earth	cardinal
Point 8	Pisces	water	mutable
Point 9	Aries	fire	cardinal

In the hexagram the three astrological qualities of fixed, cardinal and mutable alternate twice with each other, while the divine triangle passes once through each of these three qualities – but each time in a different sequence.

Here we have, then, the cosmic relationships, both of the planets and the zodiac, which the Enneagram can order and illuminate for us.

It should also have become clear how the laws of Creation and the cosmos are reflected in the Enneagram, which can therefore truly be seen as a cosmic symbol of formative, creative forces.

Notes

1   These much-quoted tablets were either lost or only existed in legend. The text quoted here is taken from Levi, Eliaphas, *Schlüssel zu den grossen Mysterien*.

2   Cf for more details of these correspondences: Vollmar, Klausbernd, *Journey Through the Chakras*. Also: Vollmar, Klausbernd, *Chakren – Lebenskraft und Lebensfreude aus der eigenen Mitte*.

3   Collin, R, *The Theory of Celestial Influence*, page 51.

4   Norelli-Bachelet, P, *The Gnostic Circle*.

5   In the system of secondary progressions when analysing a birth horoscope, both the moon and Saturn require 29 years for a complete orbit through the zodiac.

6   The sidereal orbit periods of the planets show clearly why we distinguish between personal and transpersonal planets. The personal planets, as far as Saturn, return to the same place in the zodiac many times in the life of a single human being. The sidereal orbit of Mercury takes 0.24 years (about 3 months); that of Venus 0.6 years (about 7 months); the earth of course takes one year; Mars takes 1.88 years; Jupiter 11.86 years; and Saturn 29.5 years. The transpersonal planets from Uranus to Pluto rarely return to the same place in the lifetime of one person. The sidereal orbit of Uranus takes about 84 years, that of Neptune almost 165 years, and that of Pluto 248.43 years.

7   Cf for more details on this: Sicuteri, Roberto, *Astrologie und Mythos. Mythen und Symbole im Spiegel der Tiefenpsychologie*.

8   According to Rodney Collin *(The Theory of Celestial Influence*, page 112), the power of attraction of the moon is so great because it is greatly magnified by the small diameter of the human blood vessels.

9   Collin, R, *The Theory of Celestial Influence*, page 112.

10   Jung, E and von Franz, M-L, *Grail Legend*.

11   Neumann, Erich, *Ursprungsgeschichte des Bewusstseins*, M Fischer, Frankfurt, 1984. Neumann speaks here especially about the fear of the male principle of being sucked back into the unconscious feminine (which is also the creative principle).

12   Its distance from the earth varies between 88 and 640 million kilometers within 16 years.

13   Cf for more detail, the excellent work by the anthroposophist Joachim Schultz, *Rythmen der Sterne. Erscheinungen und Bewegungen von Sonne, Mond und Planeten*. The movements of Mars have both periodic and spatial irregularities and variations of a kind not encountered in any other planet of our solar system.

14   Norelli-Bachelet, P, *The Gnostic Circle*.

15   The name Kali derives from the root 'kala' which means 'time' in Sanskrit.

16   Cf for more detail, the excellent book by Jung's pupil, Kerenyi, Karl, *Die Mythologie der Griechen, Vol. 1*.

17   Sicuteri, Roberto, *Astrologie und Mythos*.

18   Norelli-Bachelet, P, *The Gnostic Circle*.

19   I have never managed to properly understand this WHEEL system, which was hardly known beyond the circle of Graf Keyserling. Whoever would like to find out more, should look at the book I have mentioned already: Neue Wiener Shule, *Im Jahr des Uranus*. On the illustration between pages 128 and 129, the reader will find a coloured depiction of the WHEEL, which can also be obtained as a poster from the publisher. On the Enneagram one can find more information in: Keyserling, Arnold Graf, *Klaviatur des Denkens*, Vienna, self-published.

CHAPTER 7

Synthesis: An Overview of the Enneagram

Do not think, but look.

Ludwig Wittgenstein

Having arrived at Enneagram point 7 of this book, at its goal, I would now like to provide a brief overview of the many interpretative possibilities the Enneagram contains. When looking at the following tables, we can recognize the various character types and action strategies which the Enneagram embodies. Ultimately, these elements which we assign to the Enneagram's nine points are the expressions of cosmic being; they represent variations of one and the same creative power. By studying the Enneagram, we can become more consciously aware of our place within this cosmic being.

A

I third: the material preconditions of a process
The outer conditions are recognized, the material foundations considered

Enneagram point 1 the material conditions	outward perception	the 'Entrepreneur'
Enneagram point 2 analysis of the material conditions	love of action	the 'Planner'
Enneagram point 3 (mechanical shock point): a new external impulse keeps the process on track	new quality: the psyche	the 'Magician'

II third: the material to be transformed through the process
The changes necessary to keep the process properly directed

Enneagram point 4 striving forward	overcoming obstacles with difficulty	the 'Emotional Person'
Enneagram point 5 directing one's efforts towards a goal	doubt that one will reach one's goal, suffering	the 'Observer'
Enneagram point 6 (conscious shock point): a new external impulse directs the process towards its goal	new quality: the mind/intellect	the 'Hero'

III third: the aim and purpose of the 'work'
The process is successfully completed

Enneagram point 7 coming close to the goal	representation to the outer world	the 'Optimist'
Enneagram point 8 the goal is finally attained	reason and intelligence	the 'Mediator'
Enneagram point 9 (third shock point): new beginning	new quality: the higher self (the body)	the 'Loving One'

B

I third: Typical characteristics: body-orientated, mechanical/motor reaction patterns, fast speed

Base chakra (Muladhara)	Mercury (Hermes)	Violet	Taurus
Sex chakra (Svadhishthana)	Venus (Aphrodite)	Violet	Cancer
Solar plexus chakra (Manipura, Hara)	Earth/Moon	Blue	Leo

II third: Typical characteristics: feeling-orientated, emotional reaction patterns, medium speed

Solar plexus chakra (Manipura, Hara)	Mars (Apollo)	Green	Virgo
Heart chakra (Anahata)	Jupiter (Zeus)	Green	Scorpio
Heart chakra (Anahata)	Saturn (Chronos)	Yellow	Sagittarius

III third. Typical characteristics: mind-orientated, intellectual reaction patterns, slowness

Throat chakra (Vishuddha)	Uranus (Uranos)	Orange	Capricorn
Third Eye (Ajna)	Neptune (Poseidon)	Orange	Pisces
Crown chakra (Sahasrara)	Pluto (Hades)	Red	Aries

Looking at this table, one can see that action-strategies, psychological types, chakras, planets, colours and zodiac signs all augment each other and provide us with a whole picture for each Enneagram point. They show us different aspects, as it were, of the essence of an Enneagram point.

If we look at Enneagram point 1, the colour violet, as the darkest colour of the spectrum, shows us that we are at the beginning of our journey and do not yet see either our path or our goal clearly. We are fully involved with external things, living through our base chakra which regulates the physical and material aspect of our life. The American psychologist Abraham Maslow says that the first stage of human motivation is mainly to do with survival. This is the foundation upon which any higher development can be built. At this beginning stage we find Mercury, the patron of tradesmen and thieves, who is himself not yet a god.

Once basic material necessity has been catered for, we are still involved in our material needs at Enneagram point 2. Violet still holds sway, symbolizing the perspective towards darkness. But in spite of this close-knit connection with the material realm, divine power appears at this stage in the shape of Venus, who helps us to form and shape our material circumstances and surroundings in an aesthetic way. We grace the physical with beauty, and so can overcome it. Our actions are informed by the world of the sex chakra. At Enneagram point 2, attraction and enticement rule, which are always functions of beauty.

The colour blue at Enneagram point 3 leads us towards the light. Through external help we become aware that the psyche exists in addition to the material world. What was prepared in us by the sex chakra, now blossoms: we discover our feelings, moods and emotions, which are characteristically ruled by the moon. The 'Magician' is at home in this domain; he knows how to work with the human power of imagination, and how, apparently, to master the physical realm.

At Enneagram points 3 and 4 we are influenced by the solar plexus chakra; this teaches us how to deal with our negative feelings – which are among the greatest obstacles on our path towards perfection. At Enneagram point 4, under the influence of Mars, we ask ourselves how we should get to grips with our own aggression and barriers. The colour green can give us the answer we need: we must strive to bring light and dark into harmony with each other, as green demonstrates to us in its balanced mixing of yellow (representative of light) and blue (representative of dark). By creating this harmony we can overcome our own hindrances, can integrate our shadow and, as 'emotional' people, come a step closer to our goal.

This brings us to the realm of the heart chakra, also ruled by the colour green. At Enneagram point 5, Jupiter helps us to resolve the suffering we experienced in the tension between light and darkness, and to concentrate all our efforts on the attainment of our goal. Yet we must still continue to battle with doubt, which makes us think our goal is out of reach. The positive power of Jupiter is, ultimately, stronger, and allows us to overcome our suffering and reach the second shock-point stage.

At Enneagram point 6 we enter the light (yellow), the intellectual realm of the Enneagram. At this point the 'Hero' – with external help – crosses the threshold between subjective and objective, between personal and transpersonal realms. Cleansed by Saturn of his limited, egotistic viewpoint, the seeker arrives at his goal at Enneagram point 7.

The 'Optimist' is well placed to give voice to his success, since both the throat chakra and Uranus help him to blow his own trumpet. The warmth of orange shows that the 'Optimist' is by no means just a self-seeking egotist; in spite of his extrovert nature, he has a great deal of sympathy for others. But at Enneagram point 7, nevertheless, the goal has been attained only in a superficial form.

The 'Mediator', finally, arrives at his ultimate goal at Enneagram point 8 by means of his intelligence and reason, and also, not least, through the power of the Third Eye. As the 'Loving One' he makes the transition at Enneagram point 9 to the beginning of a new cycle. Here, at the apex of the Enneagram, red stands – as it does in Goethe's colour theory – for the intensification of all other colours. Here we find the higher self, the highest aspect of all our human striving. The subtle, transcending influence of Pluto is at work here.

The zodiac signs do not combine quite so seamlessly with the 'table of elements' of the separate Enneagram points. For me they represent a distinct cycle, which nevertheless possesses a perfect inner consistency and enables it to find full reflection in the Enneagram.

Afterword

At the very moment that I think I know all the answers to life, all my questions about life suddenly change.

Saul Kuchinsky

I have now described various different aspects of the cosmic symbol of the Enneagram. But that is not to say that the themes I have chosen have exhausted the Enneagram's potential. As I said at the beginning of the book, every dynamic process can be organized and analysed by means of it. All I have done is to search out and describe a few salient themes and processes so as to clarify both the Enneagram's logic and the teachings of Gurdjieff. Even though Gurdjieff's esoteric teachings may now be enjoying something of a fashionable revival, their content is still relatively unknown. I hope that this book will have helped to redress this situation. Since the Enneagram teaching occupies a central place in Gurdjieff's system of ideas, all that I have described can also be seen as an introduction to his world view. After reading this book you should be able to draw up Enneagrams yourself for your own purposes. The 'work' with the Enneagram will expand your perception. It is both a model of, and help with, the processes of understanding; and, like all Gurdjieff's teachings, eminently practical. It really should, if possible, be used and applied every day; you will only fathom the real depths of the Enneagram by using it.

Its strength lies in its capacity to answer burning questions of everyday life. Whether you can afford a new car, whether you should leave your partner or would do better to carry on living with her, what you need to do to feel better in some way – the Enneagram can clarify your situation and show you the consequences of your actions. So it can help you make decisions.

It also clearly separates and distinguishes different strands of a process and so offers ways of getting to grips with situations that may initially have seemed too complex to come to terms with. The Enneagram can open your eyes to things which you would otherwise easily overlook. It doesn't matter whether your questions are to do with your self-development or with starting a business; the Enneagram always describes nine steps with two shock points, at which external impulses influence the process.

If you wish to begin to make practical use of the Enneagram, it would be helpful to apply it to all sorts of processes, even if you already know their outcome. By doing this you will quickly develop a sense for the way a process can be ordered, and how it can be assigned in nine stages to the Enneagram points. With a little practice you will start recognizing the Enneagram pattern in any and every process; this will help you to get to grips more speedily with the underlying factors which both affect and interrupt it, and you will therefore greatly increase your confidence in making decisions and taking actions.

But in working with the Enneagram we should also not forget that life – thank goodness – is not as systematic as a superficial view of the Enneagram might seem to indicate. It seems to me that life processes are composed of a dialectic between systematic laws or sequences, and spontaneous, more or less chance occurrences. Although a systematic examination of our situation can of course help provide much greater understanding of ourselves and our surroundings, we still need to keep ourselves open for unpredictable factors.

The Enneagram, like astrology and the path of the Tarot, offers us a model for helping to take hold of life; but the multiplicity of life itself is always far more complex than the most complex model. Yet once you have understood the fundamental laws of your life, you will find it much easier to find your way back to spontaneity.

The great advantage of the Enneagram compared with other models is that it does not rely on a fixed law or a rigid system. It is a tool for developing knowledge that alters continually according to the specifics of a situation. It is a vessel that has to be filled with your own personal approach. Of course, each Enneagram point has a certain wavelength of specific characteristics, but unpredictable factors are never excluded. If you do find that you are assigning factors to Enneagram points in ways that are too fixed and unchangeable, you should question what is happening, for otherwise the system can become a rigid strait-jacket which generates nothing new. This tendency is particularly apparent in the Enneagram character typology. But if you use it carefully you will find that the typology grows and changes as you apply it. Only then can it provide ongoing stimulus to greater knowledge and understanding.

I hope it has become obvious in the course of this book that a great deal depends on how you use the Enneagram. It *can* become a mechanically applied aid that dictates to the user rather than the other way round. But used as an open, unprescribed system, it will open you to creative, intuitive solutions and points of view – to real growth and true insights.

A final word of advice for your personal use of the Enneagram: to begin with, orientate yourself according to the models and sequences I have described; but once you have accustomed yourself to these, gradually let go of them and develop your own allocation of qualities, according to your own needs and personality. In this way the Enneagram will remain for you a real and flexible tool.

I wish you much success and pleasure in your 'work' with the Enneagram.

The Practical Enneagram Test

Personality

This part of the test tells you what stage you have presently reached on your path of development, what obstacles may be in your way, and what can help you move forward. The practical Enneagram test can be applied again and again, and each time lead to different results. This is because you continually change and are confronted with different problems at different stages of your life.

A person's development can be seen in terms of a journey through nine stages. Once you have successfully completed these, you begin again on a new level, and pass once more through nine stages – and so on. You continue to evolve and develop as long as you don't get stuck in unproductive, repetitive situations. The questions in the test have the aim of making you aware of which stage in the process you are at now, and how you can develop. Just thinking about the questions can lead you to an understanding of your present circumstances and your position within the Enneagram.

The following 24 questions are not ordered in any particular sequence, and relate to the first eight Enneagram points. There are no questions relating to point 9 because it represents only a passing, transitional condition between the attainment of one's goal and entering on a new task.

The questions

1   Are you completely happy with your position or task in life?
2   Do you know what you want, and are your circumstances and surroundings helping you achieve it?
3   Have you just gained an important insight into your own life (through friends, a teacher or therapist, a book or a separation)?
4   Do you manage to observe your feelings without allowing yourself to be dominated by them?
5   Do you really want to work at the development of your personality?
6   Is a new stage in your life just beginning?
7   Are you close to attaining a (personal) objective that is important to you, and are you both glad and frightened about this success?
8   Do you feel wholly devoted to a task?
9   Are you at present looking into new possibilities for your life's path?
10   Do you usually manage to behave in a way that accords with your ideas and insights?
11   Do you find that your striving and the stress in your life is much too much for you?
12   Do people often look up to you as a role model or ideal?
13   Do you often wonder what you have so far achieved in your life?
14   Do you sometimes find life a hard grind?
15   Are you bothered by habits of yours which are a nuisance, and by sluggishness or lack of self-discipline?
16   Would you dearly like to improve your material situation?
17   Are you on the point of throwing yourself into something new?
18   Are you happy with yourself and with what you have achieved, even though you could go further with more effort?
19   Do you feel that you are stuck and not getting any further, inspite of making great efforts?

20 Do you really want to change?
21 Do you find that certain of your fellows provide particular help for your self-development?
22 Do you suffer from an inner struggle between the demands made on you and self-doubt?
23 Are you at the moment confronted by an unexpected or new external factor?
24 Do you feel that you know what the aim of your life is?

Evaluation

Search out the three questions that you can answer the most definite 'yes' to, then look at the following table to find which type your questions correspond with.

Enneagram type	Questions
1	6, 13, 17
2	9, 16, 20
3	14, 15, 19
4	3, 21, 23
5	7, 11, 22
6	2, 5, 10
7	12, 18, 24
8	1, 4, 8

Once you have found your type, mark in the following table the types for which you answered 'yes' one or more times (maximum three crosses, minimum one cross).

Enneagram type	Crosses
1	
2	
3	
4	
5	
6	
7	
8	

The types in this table correspond with the separate types of the Enneagram. Looking at this table will tell you what stage you have reached in your development. Look first at whether the types you have marked with a cross are all close to each other or are far apart.

Examples and explanations

If you tend towards just one particular type – in other words have answered 'yes' to all three questions belonging to one type – then you belong to this type without any doubt, and can immediately read the text that refers to it (in what follows, from page 194 onwards).

But it is more likely that you have put crosses next to two different types. If these follow on from one another – such as type 1 and type 2 – you are at a transitional point between the two, and should read the text that refers to each and try to understand the tension that may exist between them. You will usually find you are at a transition point from one condition of consciousness to another. Only obsessive people remain for any length of time in one single state of consciousness.

If you do the test often, you will perhaps find that sequences such as the following appear: 2, 3, 4, 2, 1, 4, 1 etc. Then you can see that you are continually moving in a circle between the first and fourth Enneagram points. That indicates a neurotic replay or repetition syndrome, such as Freud drew attention to; or otherwise mechanical, 'sleep-walking' repetitions, which Gurdjieff was so concerned to combat. Such circular motions can surface equally well on either the left- or the right-hand side of the Enneagram. Over time, the right-hand ones should settle down to a tension between point 7 and 8.

If you alternate beteen two far-distant points, then two of your egos are demanding two different things with equal vehemence. Try to understand this tension by reading through the texts which refer to each one.

If you answer 'yes' to three questions corresponding to three separate, far-distant types, then you are, without doubt, faced by an urgent decision. Do you know the feeling: 'Alas, two souls are dwelling in my breast' (Goethe's *Faust*)? Is this your present experience? Then regularly try to remember yourself, twice daily. Or are you suffering from such exhaustion that your concentration is weakened? Or perhaps one should also congratulate you on a state of creative chaos? Whichever is true, read the commentaries relating to all three types and dwell on the possible tensions and contradictions.

As well as referring to the very practically orientated texts connected with the test, I would also advise you to read about the relevant Enneagram points in the first and second chapters of this book.

Enneagram point 1

At this stage it is good to perceive your present situation as clearly as possible. See where you are at the moment and what you need to help you move on. If you keep a diary, read through the entries for the last month. You can also become aware of your present situation by observing your dreams. Try to become clear about what it is you want. Imagine this goal as clearly as possible, for visualizing your desired aim may help you. While picturing it, try to notice your feelings. Do they reject this aim or welcome it? If you are afraid of this goal, you should ponder whether it is really suitable for you.

Enneagram point 2

At this point you will be helped by finding out more about your situation from books and pamphlets etc. Gather as much information as possible and by means of this information try to become aware of the situation you are in. At the same time you should outline your aims in as clear a way as possible. Write up in detail what you want to attain and what steps are necessary to get there. Make yourself a plan – how and when will you reach your goal? Read this plan through as often as possible before falling asleep. It is also helpful to recall the past day and then to imagine what your day would have been like if your goal had already been attained.

Enneagram point 3

You have the feeling that your own strength does not really seem to help you move forward. You have probably already turned to friends for advice, perhaps you are working with a therapist or teacher. It is very important at this point to find some form of external help, someone to whom you can open yourself fully. It is false pride to think that you can do everything on your own. Part of your development consists in being able to accept that you need external help. Accept such support gratefully. You have the chance to learn something about humility. You should regularly practise self-remembering.

Enneagram point 4

It is very likely that you are struggling with your emotions, and have difficulty in practising therapeutic or spiritual exercises with any regularity. Try to observe very precisely in what areas you lack will and self-discipline. Try to remember yourself for a few minutes each day. Do not let yourself fall back into old patterns of behaviour, even if you are unhappy with your present situation. Observe how your old forms of behaviour rule you and make you discontent. Do not break off therapy at this stage or give up your teacher; do not withdraw from your friendships. Experiment consciously with new patterns of reaction and behaviour, and observe what inward effect they have on you. Keep a diary in which you note down your moods, and try to keep your goal clearly before you.

Enneagram point 5

You are often unhappy at this stage and suffer from the fact that you have still not attained your goal. Have patience! This suffering is necessary for your development, since it mobilizes all your forces. You have come to the point at which the only possible path for you is the way forward towards your goal. Try to understand your experiences and observe yourself with a certain objectivity. Do not withdraw too much – stay within reach of the people around you. Try, as far as possible, to orientate your whole life towards your goal. You may have to sacrifice certain things, but it will be worth it in the end.

Enneagram point 6

It is likely that at this stage the external world once more assumes great importance for you. Open yourself to what comes towards you from without. Look carefully at how you can make conscious use of such factors. Try, if possible every evening before you go to sleep, to visualize and then write down what you have learnt from others during the course of the past day. Set yourself little goals on the path towards your final goal. Notice how this strengthens your will. Write down your transitional goals on a piece of paper that you carry with you wherever you go, so that you can be continually reminded what you are aiming for.

Enneagram point 7

Congratulations! You have reached your goal. Your will has been strengthened and you now manage to live more or less as you would like. You can be pleased with your achievement, and initially at least, enjoy the freedom you have attained. New tasks will come towards you soon enough. But you can also decide to give yourself wholly to your attained goal. It is always possible to go a little further and become more perfect! You are now in a position to make a clear decision about the future course of your life. Make this decision consciously. In Gurdjieff's terms, you have woken from sleep and become a responsible, adult human being. Sense the freedom which a conscious decision brings you. It will help you continue to remember yourself regularly and to experience new dimensions of this exercise.

Enneagram point 8

You have learnt to serve a task or a cause. Continue to devote yourself as fully as possible to this service. Give yourself to it. Any further advice would be inappropriate here. You yourself will notice at what point you should move on again to a new level of the task you have completed, and when a new task claims your attention and interest.

Business and finance

Bennett, in particular, drew attention to the fact that the nine stages of the Enneagram should be viewed as developmental steps in a process or situation that build upon each other. Every process must pass through these nine stages in order to reach fulfilment and provide the basis for new processes to take place. If you are unsure why a business or financial undertaking is not running according to plan, you can apply the following test. Evaluating the results will give you ideas about what to do to remedy the situation.

Since financial and production processes are so many and various, a questionnaire in the form of a test would either be too lengthy or too general to provide a useful diagnostic tool. Instead, I have drawn up a list of questions that is easy to use and which will facilitate your analysis of economic processes and help you to come to decisions. This list is useful not only for the professional management of businesses, but also for helping to structure daily, personal work processes in a clearer and more efficient way.

If you wish to start a new area of work or a business, or if you want to change the way your business operates, it is best to read one after another all the observations and questions relating to all nine of the Enneagram points. If you are analysing problems in a business which already exists, please first answer the following questions either with 'yes' or 'no'.

1 Do you consider your business to be inadequately provided with either technology or finances? (If the answer is 'yes', read the commentary to Enneagram point 1 and perhaps also point 7.)
2 Do you have difficulties in organizing the work? (If 'yes', read the commentary on Enneagram points 2 and 4, and perhaps also 5.)
3 Are your products or services not marketable enough? (If 'yes', read the commentary on Enneagram points 3, 6 and 7, and perhaps also 5.)
4 Do you have advertising problems? (If 'yes', read the commentary on Enneagram points 6 and 7.)
5 Do you have marketing and sales problems? (If 'yes', read the commentary on Enneagram point 8.)

Enneagram point 1

Be clear first of all what material supplies and conditions are available to you. Draw up a list of factors you already have which could help make production processes easier. Include your own abilities, training and experiences, as well as your financial situation. This list can help you form ideas about a project or service you might offer, or about how to make your present work easier. If you already have an idea for the marketing of a product or service, ask yourself what material conditions are lacking at the moment to ease the work process and make it more viable.

1 When you look at your financial goal, do you think that you have a problem as regards your available capital or equipment? Yes or no?
2 Do you think that your capacities, experiences and training are sufficient to allow you to attain your financial goal? Yes or no?

If you have answered both the above questions with 'no', you should alter your goal and make it more compatible with what is available to you.

If you have answered both questions with 'yes', you can proceed to Enneagram point 2.

Enneagram point 2

Once you have analysed your material conditions and your abilities, you need to apply and coordinate them so that you can attain your aim in as rational a way as possible. Analyse how you can best make use of your technical aids so that you can be most effective and lose least time. Draw up a logical, rational plan of the sequence of your work processes, so that all your available capacities are used to the full.

1   Do you feel that there are too many slack or idle times in the production process? Yes or no?
2   Do you think that following your work plan would overtax and stress you? Yes or no?

If you have answered both questions with 'yes', you should take a long hard look at your work plan and seek for creative solutions for coordinating your material conditions in a rather more rational way. Experience shows that it is very important to visualize a planned production or work sequence with as much clarity as possible.

If you have answered both questions with 'no', then no further analysis is necessary, and you can proceed to Enneagram point 3.

Enneagram point 3

Once you have clarified your material conditions and organization, you must turn your attention to your product or service. Consider what product or work will be most successful given your circumstances. Here, at Enneagram point 3, you need an impetus, a catchy idea that can prevail in current market conditions. It is likely, therefore, that you will need advice from an external source. It is up to you whether this takes the form of management consultants or whether you just study the reports of industries and businesses operating in the same field. What is important is to have an exciting and workable concept that corresponds wih your abilities and individual situation.

1 Do you think that you do not have such a concept, that you do not know what to do with your available capacities? Yes or no?
2 Are there many other people who already offer the product or services you are considering? Yes or no?

If you have answered one or both questions with 'yes', then find yourself a really good professional adviser. The better he is, the better are your chances of success. Experience has shown that people often try to make false savings at this point. Being too circumspect at the outset can cost you dearly later on.

If you have answered 'no' to the second question, think about the reasons why there are few other suppliers of your product or services.

If you answer 'no' to both questions, or if you are not troubled by the reasons for there being few other suppliers of the service or product you want to offer, you can proceed to Enneagram point 4.

Enneagram point 4

Up to now your considerations have been largely theoretical; now we need to look at the concrete factors in the production or work process.

1 Where are there obstacles in the actual process of production, or in the organization of the service you are offering?
2 Where are there tensions and difficulties in the actual organization of the work?

To overcome or lessen such obstacles, it will often be necessary to return to the more abstract considerations of Enneagram points 1 and 2, and to draw the appropriate conclusions on the basis of the practical experience you have now acquired.

If there are no obstacles in the production process or organization (which is rare), you can proceed without further analysis or restructuring to Enneagram point 5.

Enneagram point 5

All the experiences you have had up to now can allow you, at Enneagram point 5, to have a clear view of the goal you are aiming for, with all its consequences. You are now in a position to coordinate your production system exactly with your product, or your organization with the service you offer. This usually leads at this stage to a modification of your goal. You must be clear that the best laid economic plans are of little use if they are not based carefully and precisely on your production system.

At Enneagram point 3 we looked at the theoretical production idea; now we must be flexible enough to accommodate this idea to the reality of our production system. This often presents psychological hurdles. One can feel that one's original idea is being betrayed because of external factors.

Is the product carefully based on the available production conditions? Yes or no?

If you answer 'no', you must either change these conditions or change your product or service. If you want to change the underlying conditions and parameters, look again carefully at Enneagram point 4. If you wish to change your product or service (which is easier), draw up a list of the ways in which your production and work parameters affect your product. Analysing this list should give you ideas for modifying your product or service.

If you have answered 'yes', you can proceed to the sixth Enneagram point.

Enneagram point 6

At this stage of the process you need to give a final honing and polish to your product or service. One could also call it 'styling'. What sort of philosophical or ideological relationship do you wish to have with your product or service? You need to formulate and present a suitable image for your business. You must consider what questions are currently surfacing in the society around you (and in particular in your prospective circle of clients). Remember that nowadays every product also embodies a certain way of life. It will be helpful to look back once more to Enneagram point 3, to review your original production idea.

At this stage you can, ultimately, ask yourself what the social purpose of your product or service is. Draw up a list which shows how your business connects with current debate about new social forms. Aspects particularly worthy of consideration are ecology and self-development.

1 Does my product/service serve the society in which I live? Yes or no?
2 Does my product/service convey a particular lifestyle or a new quality? Yes or no?

If you answer 'no' to either of these, it is worth returning to Enneagram point 3.

If you answer 'yes' to both, you can proceed to Enneagram point 7.

Enneagram point 7

Now, at last, you can present your product/service to the outside world. You encounter the question of advertising and communication.

Is my product/service known to all potential buyers? Yes or no?

If you answer 'no', you should take another look at Enneagram point 1, to help you decide what financial outlay you can afford to invest in advertising; also Enneagram point 6, so as to take advertising considerations into account at that point.

It is often helpful at this stage to draw up an advertising Enneagram, especially if you think that this represents the weak point of your business.

If you answered 'yes', you can proceed to Enneagram point 8.

Enneagram point 8

At Enneagram point 8 you can consider your product itself. To help organize the sale of goods more effectively, it may be worth drawing up a further Enneagram.

Once you have achieved good sales organization, you have arrived at your goal.

Enneagram point 9

At this point you can think about whether it is appropriate to develop a new follow-up product.

Who were Gurdjieff, Ouspensky and Bennett?

George Ivanovich Gurdjieff

Gurdjieff (sometimes written Gurdjeff), probably the eldest of six brothers and sisters, was born in January 1866 (or possibly 1865) in Asia Minor, in the Greek quarter of the Russian town Alexandropolis (in Armenia). He died at 10.30am on the 29 October 1949 in the American hospital at Neuilly near Paris.

Gurdjieff is certainly one of the most intriguing and fascinating teachers of our century. He appeared in manifold guises, as dance teacher, magician, carpet and antiques dealer, hypnotist, writer and pedagogue. He influenced many famous artists of his time, such as the writers Aldous Huxley (1894–1963) and D H Lawrence (1885–1930), the American architect Frank Lloyd Wright (1869–1959), the Jewish writer Arthur Koestler (1905–1983) as well as the Australian writer Katherine Mansfield (pseudonym for Kathleen Beauchamp, 1888–1923) who died in his institute in Fontainebleau.

Gurdjieff's much-loved father Giorgios Giorgiades was a so-called 'Ashokh', one of the last bards of his area, who could still sing the old legends and folk tales. Giorgiades fell into poverty and moved with his family to Kars, where the young Gurdjieff was instructed in strict theological dogma. He was very much impressed by orthodox Christianity. After various adventures as a youth, in which he encountered paranormal phenomena and was nearly frightened to death, he came upon the teachings of the Dervishes and Sufis in 1885. These teachings, which he later studied still more intensively, continued to influence and inform his views until his death. Gurdjieff can be seen as the first teacher to make the guarded secrets of the Sufis accessible to a large number of Western seekers.

In 1886, as he recounts, he discovered indications about the Enneagram for the first time, and about the supposed Sarmoun Brotherhood. He set out on a search for their monastery, which took him to (among other places) Egypt, Ethiopia, the Sudan, Iraq, and also to Mecca and Medina. As an agent of the Russian Czar, he travelled to India and Tibet. In 1898, he apparently discovered the Sarmoun Brotherhood's chief monastery, in which he received deep insights into the Enneagram teachings and sacred dances. From then on, the Enneagram became an intrinsic part of his teachings about the need for human beings to wake up. Before he married Julia Ostrowska in 1912 and read Ouspensky's *Tertium Organum*, he occupied himself intensively with Persian magic and Lamaistic Buddhism, which he studied in Tibet.

In Moscow and St Petersburg Gurdjieff founded his first groups, in which he taught extensively about the Enneagram. In 1915, Ouspensky joined these groups. In the following years, up to 1919, his most loyal pupils joined him, such as Thomas and Olga de Hartmann, and Alexander and Jeanne (de) Salzmann. Ouspensky, in the meantime, had distanced himself from Gurdjieff, as he had done so once before.

In 1921, Gurdjieff was invited to the institute, at Hellerau near Dresden, of the Austrian movement teacher Emile Jacques-Dalcroze (1865–1950), the founder of eurythmics. In the same year he met Bennett, whom he encouraged to work with the Enneagram.

Gurdjieff travelled to Germany and on the 24 November 1921 held an introductory lecture on his system. But he was not allowed to remain in Hellerau for legal reasons. In the following year, Olga de Hartmann founded the Prieuré de Basses Loges in Fontainebleau for him, where he opened his famous institute and started to work intensively on the 'movements'. He became better and better known, visiting the USA ten times, where Alfred Richard Orage, who had previously published the literary periodical *New Age*, helped him acquire a large circle of pupils. The Fontainebleau institute quickly became known worldwide as a centre for 'rustic philosophers'.

At the end of 1924, Gurdjieff began work on his chief opus, *Beelzebub's Tales To His Grandson*, which he sent for publication shortly before his death. When, in 1926, the English sex-magician and writer Aleister Crowley visited the institute, Gurdjieff unceremoniously threw him out.

The institute fell into financial difficulties and had to close in 1933; from then on, Gurdjieff's group met in his small Paris flat. From 1940 onwards, Jeanne Salzmann led her own group in Paris; this exerted increasing influence and, after Gurdjieff's death, carried on his work. Shortly before his death in 1949, Gurdjieff gave Jeanne Salzmann the legacy of his last instructions and plans for the group.

After Ouspensky's death at the end of 1947, his widow advised her husband's pupils to join Gurdjieff's group. In the same year, Bennett was officially appointed to Gurdjieff's study group, and became, together with René Zuber and Lord Pentland, one of the editors of *Beelzebub's Tales*.

The autobiographical material we have is *Meetings With Remarkable Men* (which tells of the first part of his life) and *Life is Real Only Then, When 'I Am'* (the first section of which describes Gurdjieff's middle period).

Peter Demian Ouspensky

Peter Demian (or Piotr Demianovich) Ouspensky was born in 1877 in Moscow, and died in London in 1947. He was a mathematician and scientist, and a very successful writer and journalist. He discovered his interest in literature at an early age, and in 1905 published *The Strange Life of Ivan Osokin*, which is concerned with the way things continually recur and repeat in the same compulsive way.

After extended journeys to Egypt and the Orient, he took up residence in St Petersburg and began, in addition to his work as a writer, to hold popular lectures. After writing *The Fourth Way* in 1909, he published, in 1911, his philosophical work *Tertium Organum*, which is based on the 1st Organum (meaning 'tool' or 'aid' in Latin) of Aristotle, and the 2nd Organum of Francis Bacon. Gurdjieff read this work with great interest. But Ouspensky did not meet Gurdjieff until the spring of 1915, at his St Petersburg group, when he returned to Moscow from his travels to Ceylon and India, where he had met, among others, the spiritual teacher Sri Aurobindo (Aurobindo Ghose, 1872–1950), who also worked with the Enneagram.

Ouspensky was immediately fascinated by Gurdjieff. It was he, Ouspensky, who brought him wide recognition, drawing on his many contacts and connections with intellectual and theosophical circles in Moscow and St Petersburg.

In 1920, Ouspensky went to Constantinople to lead a study group of his own. From 1921 until his death, he was a most popular and successful teacher in London and the USA.

For eight years Ouspensky retained a more or less close contact with Gurdjieff; from 1915 to 1918, they worked intensively together. Ouspensky formed Gurdjieff's teaching, which was very similar to his own, into a systematic whole; as a scientist he was particularly interested in Gurdjieff's complex system of transmuting substances (hydrogen and carbon tables), to which he applied the Enneagram. He was the first person to publicize Gurdjieff's teaching – in particular about the Enneagram – in his book *In Search of the Miraculous*.

Around 1919, the two started to go their own different ways: Ouspensky's particular aim was to study the human being's potential for development. He worked out a psychology of freedom which is somewhat similar to that of Krishnamurti (Juddu Nariahna).

After Ouspensky's death, his pupils became followers of Gurdjieff, Bennett and Jeanne Salzmann.

John Godolphin Bennett

Bennett was born on the 8 June 1877 and died in December 1974. Like Gurdjieff, he had near-death experiences – both in war and in his later years – which greatly influenced him.

It is no exaggeration to say that he was a universal genius. He was a mathematician and for a long time the director of an industrial research institute that investigated the chemistry of carbon. He was also an English spy, who studied Asiatic languages and religions, was particularly knowledgeable about Islam and travelled extensively in the Middle and Far East. He studied the books of the founder of the esoteric Arcan school and the Lucis Trust, Alice A Bailey (1880–1949), and himself wrote many books which are influenced by the work of Gurdjieff and Ouspensky.

In 1920, Bennett got to know Gurdjieff and Ouspensky. It was he who persuaded Gurdjieff to come to Europe. He maintained an intermittent contact with both Gurdjieff and Ouspensky up until the latter's death. In 1948, he became an official member of the Gurdjieff group in Fontainebleau, an acknowledged pupil of Gurdjieff and co-editor of *Beelzebub's Tales To His Grandson*. Previous to this he had purchased Coombe Springs, his research laboratory near London, and transformed it into an 'Institute for the Comparative Study of History, Philosophy and Science'. There he built up a fast-expanding group. A few years before his death he left Coombe Springs to found the 'International Academy for Education' at Sherborne House in Gloucestershire. Here, from October 1971 to December 1974, he held lectures on, among other things, the principles underlying the Enneagram; he also inspired the study group 'Systematics', which was concerned with the application of the Enneagram teachings to business management.

Bennett's aim at Coombe Springs, and even more so at Sherborne House, was to develop independent communities which worked upon the inner development of each individual; he thought these were the only kind which could survive the chaotic times he believed were fast approaching. Like modern evolution theorists Bennett thought that working towards our own transformation is absolutely necessary, given the huge disturbances and revolutions of our time. He strove to teach how we can take responsibility for ourselves and how to use daily life as our esoteric school.

Sherborne House no longer exists, but Bennett also inspired a similar project in Claymont (West Virginia, USA) that survived him. This institute was directed for ten years by Pierre Elliott, a teacher of the 'movements'.

In the fifties, Bennett was visited at Coombe Springs by Pak Subuh (Muhammed Subuh, who had founded a brotherhood in Indonesia in 1947 to teach gymnastic exercises which lead to ecstatic states). In Subud, the movement based on Subuh's work, Bennett recognized a path to the realization of true Christianity, which had also been the aim of both Gurdjieff and Alice A Bailey. In 1959, Bennett organized the first international Subud Congress at Coombe Springs; and until his death he remained such an active proponent of this movement that he is often regarded as its founder.

He wrote an extensive autobiography, called *Witness: The Story of a Search*, which describes his life up to the end of the fifties.

Gurdjieff's Terminology

Gurdjieff's chief work, *Beelzebub's Tales To His Grandson*, is hard to grasp partly because of the many invented words he uses, which are impenetrable unless one knows something of their origin and meaning.

I suspect that Gurdjieff partly used such unusual word-creations to get round the problem of automatic association with particular concepts. Such associations lock us into our old, habitual patterns of thought and points of view. Every word that we read and hear is coloured by all sorts of individual memories, thoughts and feelings. But Gurdjieff wished to communicate something fundamentally new, to open people's eyes. So his use of words also aims to wake them up. His vocabulary is derived from a combination of Greek, Turkish and Russian root-syllables, and tries to describe things with great precision from as many different aspects as possible. Gurdjieff aims, like the post-modernists, for a holistic view not based on old, well-worn associations.

To facilitate the reading of *Beelzebub's Tales*, I have included the following glossary, which lists Gurdjieff's most important concepts. It is very helpful to have it next to you as you read his book.

The elements of the Enneagram as represented in *Beelzebub's Tales*

Triamasikamno: the Law of Three

Harnelmiatznell: also expresses the Law of Three, which says that the higher principle welds together with the lower to produce the middle realm

Surp-Otheos: the positive or active force

Surp-Skiros: the negative or passive force

Surp-Athanatos: the neutral or binding force

Mdnel-In: the three shock points

Mechanically occurring Mdnel-In: the mechanical shock point at Enneagram point 3

Intentionally realized Mdnel-In: the conscious shock point at Enneagram point 6

Eftalogodiksis or *Heptaparaparschinoch*: the Law of Seven

Tasaluninono: the seven aspects of every phenomenon

Protoächari: Enneagram point 1

Deuteroächari: Enneagram point 2

Tritoächari: Enneagram point 4

Tetaroächari or *Harnelahut*: Enneagram point 5 (also used to describe the transition between point 4 and point 5)

Piandschoächari: Enneagram point 7

Exioächari: Enneagram point 8

Resulsarion: Enneagram point 9

Partkdolg-duty: the conscious 'work' of self-remembering in order to awaken, which is connected with intentional suffering, since we must battle with the sluggishness of our own nature

Heropass: time or process in time

Other important concepts in alphabetical order

Abdest: washing of the genitals

Adiat (Haida): fashion

Almnoschinu: materializing the reason or other function of a dead person in order to communicate with him

Anaschi: hashish

Ansabaluiazar: transformation or mutual interaction of energies

Anstruarhelt: nervousness

Antkuano: the automatic perfection of reason in the realm of time

Askokin: food for the moon (our unconscious nature) which is formed from the disintegration of living substance

Ätherogram: comparable to a telegram

Ätherokrilno: the cosmic substance of divine nature

Blagonurarinian feeling: pricks of conscience

Bulmarschano: a form of information current in the ancient continent of Atlantis, corresponding to our present-day books

Chirnuanovo: alteration of the focal centre of the solar system

Darthelchlustnian condition: a state in which one hearkens to one's inner experiences (a kind of meditation)

Dianosk: day

Diapharon: sport

Dimtzoniro: obligation to keep a promise (one has made to one-self)

Dschartklom: light and darkness, pricks of conscience, the separation of the negating, affirming and uniting force

Dscherimetli: materialization of the soul of a dead person

Ekbarzerbation: lead people astray

Exioächari: sperm

Ganbledsoin: magnetism in the sense of Franz Mesmer; also blood

Gasometronolturiko: physiology

Hammam: sacrificial offering

Hasnamus: an unprincipled, egotistic person, who nevertheless sets himself clear goals

Hawatwernomi: religion

Hernasdschena: family tree

Hichdschnapar: sympathy

Ikriltaskara: the capacity to pursue particular associations consciously

Instruaric: nervous

Irodohahun: the general life-principle of human beings
Jaboliunosar: (religiosity), nervousness
Jamtesternoche: teachings
Kalkaki: (spiritual) teachings
Kaltane (Sakrupiake): restaurant
Kaschiraitlir: book (parchment), manifesto
Kedschan-body: the second body of the human being, which is seen as being of very fine substance and spiritualized.
Keva: chewing gum
Khalqa: Group (in the Sufi tradition of a group of people who work spiritually towards their perfection)
Khlarfogo: pricks of conscience
Krhrrhihirchi: dynamo
Kroanen: sacrificial offerings
Kscherknar: a kind of searching for vision, meditation
Kschtawatcht: incite
Kundabuffer: an organ introduced temporarily into the human being to stop him perceiving his reality. It creates falsehood and blindness
Latinaki: shepherds
Logomonismus: knowledge from past times, that is passed on by initiates
Martfotai: true individuality (as attained from the sixth Ennea-gram point onwards)
Murdurten: onanism
Nichtsunnichtono: everything is dissolved into primal substance
Nipilhuatschi: the river Nile
Oblekiunerisch: horoscope
Okidanoch: will-power
Ornakr: month
Oskianer: educator
Oskiano: education
Oskolniku: gratitude
Otkaluparnish: unpleasant
Perambarsasidaan: tuning fork
Prosphora: bread
Pythien (Tiklunien): media (derived from the Delphic Oracle)

Raskuarno: the separation of single cells from the whole, death

Rastropunilo: smell

Rollenkandelnost: stimulus to, or capacity for, association

Sakrupiake (Kaltane): restaurant

Sakukinolturiko: hypnosis

Samonolturiko: medicine

Satkein: poison gas

Semzekionic: burdensome

Similisiernic: allegorical

Sinkrpussaren: belief in the products of the imagination

Sitritt: Caesarian section

Soliunenensis: planetary tensions which affect human feelings

Spezitualitivic condensing: the brain

Sunniat: cutting back

Sustat: consciousness

Teleokrimalnic thought-waves: corresponds roughly to the morphogenetic fields described by Rupert Sheldrake

Tenikdoa: law of gravity

Teskkuano: telescope

Tetartokosmos: animal

Theomertmologos: creative impulse

Tikliamian: Sumerian: according to Gurdjieff the highest degree of culture ever attained by humanity

Tiklunien (Pythien): (trance-)medium

Tirzikiano: lamp

Trogautoegocratic process: one in which the human being unconsciously serves the moon (his unconscious nature). By so doing he nourishes the moon. (The literal meaning of the word is: I hold myself together by eating)

Tschakla: hemp

Turinurino: constancy

Tuspuschok: appendix

Tüssy: abortion

Urnel: show off (exaggerate)

Valikrin: introduce the blood of a living person into the body of a dead person

Vibroechonitansko (Khlarfogo): pricks of conscience
Winduretznel: external phenomenon
Zerlikner: doctor

Bibliography

The quotes from Anthony G E Blake at the beginning of some chapters come from his brilliant book: Blake, Anthony G E, *Intelligent Enneagram*, Shambhala, Boulder/London, 1996. The quote from Rodney Collin at the beginning of Chapter 3 is taken from: Collin, Rodney, *Spiegel des Lichts*, Plejaden, Boltersen, 1990. The quote from Kuchinsky comes from: Kuchinsky, Saul, *Systematics. Search for Miraculous Management*, Claymont Communication, Charles Town, West Virginia, 1987. The Gurdjieff quotes at the beginning of chapters 4 and 6 come from: Ouspensky, P D, *In Search of the Miraculous*, Routledge and Kegan Paul, London, 1957; the Gurdjieff quote at the beginning of Chapter 5 comes from *Beelzebub's Tales To His Grandson*.

In the list that follows I have only included those books which I have referred to when writing this book, and which I think are important for a study of the Fourth Way. The works of Gurdjieff are listed in the order in which he wrote them.

I would also like to draw your attention to the American periodical: *Enneagram Educator*, West Morse Avenue, Chicago/III 60645. This reports on the Enneagram's application to the realm of psychology and community work, from a mainly Christian standpoint.

Anderson, Margaret, *The Fiery Fountains*, Rider & Co., London, 1953
——*The Unknowable Gurdjieff*, Routledge & Kegan Paul, London, 1962 (This book is very influenced by Orage; it

describes Gurdjieff's teachings in a rather brief and occasionally opaque manner.)

Anon, *Guide and Index to All and Everything: Beelzebub's Tales To His Grandson*, Traditional Studies Press, Toronto, 1973

Beesing, Maria, Nogosek, Robert J, and O'Leary, Patrick H, *The Enneagram: A Journey of Self-Discovery*, Dimension Books, Denville/New York, 1983

Bennett, John Godolphin, *What Are We Living For?* Hodder and Stoughton, London, 1949

——*Witness. The Story of a Search*, Hodder and Stoughton, London, 1962

——*Gurdjieff – A Great Enigma*, Coombe Springs Press, Ripon, 1969

——*Making a New World*, Turnstone Books, Bath, 1973

——*The Enneagram. Transformation of Man Series No. 2*, Coombe Springs Press, Ripon, 1974 (expanded edition: *Enneagram Studies*, Samuel Weiser, York Beach, 1983)

——*How We Do Things*, Coombe Springs Press, Ripon, 1965

——*Talks on Beelzebub's Tales*, Weiser, US, 1988

——*Transformation*, Coombe Springs Press, Ripon, 1982

——*HAZARD – The Risks of Realization*, Bennett Books US, Santa Fe/New Mexico, 1991

——*Is there 'Life' on Earth?*, Bennett Books, Santa Fe/New Mexico, 1989

——*Gurdjieff – der Aufbau einer neuen Welt*, Aurum, Freiburg i. Br., 1976

——*Arbiet an sich selbst. Psychologie für eine mögliche Entwicklung des Menschen*, Bruno Martin, Frankfurt (out of print)

——*Gurdjieff Heute. Seine Botschaft für ein neues Zeitalter*, Bruno Martin, Frankfurt, 1977 (out of print)

——*Harmonische Entwicklung. Gurdjieff's Psychologie der harmonischen Entwicklung des Menschen*, Bruno Martin, Südergesellen, 1982 (out of print)

——*Die inneren Welten des Menschen. Die Kosmopsychologie Gurdjieffs und der Sufis*, Bruno Martin, Südergesellen, 1984 (out of print)

——*Gurdjieff entschlüsselt. Die innere Bedeutung von Gurdjieffs*

'*Beelzebubs Erzählungen*', Bruno Martin, Frankfurt, 1976 (out of print)

Bennett, John Godolphin, *Gurdjieff – Ursprung und Hintergrund seiner Lehre*, Sphinx, Basel, 1989. (Very useful for providing a quick yet well-differentiated overview of Gurdjieff's work.)

Bennett, J G, and Bennett, Elizabeth, *Idiots in Paris: Diaries of J G and Elizabeth Bennett*, Coombe Springs Press, Ripon, 1980

Blake, Anthony G E, *Intelligent Enneagram*, Shambhala, Boulder/London, 1996. (A brilliant book that provides an original introduction, couched in modern vocabulary, into Gurdjieff's concept of intelligence.)

Bolen, Jean Shinoda, *Gods in Everyman: a new psychology of men's lives and loves*, Harper Collins, London, 1990

Butkowski-Hewitt, Anna, *With Gurdjieff in St Petersburg and Paris*, Routledge & Kegan Paul, London, 1978

Collin, Rodney, *The Theory of Celestial Influence. Man, The Universe, And Cosmic Mystery*, Shambhala, Boulder/London, 1984. (Together with the following book, this is one of the most important books on astrology/astronomy to have come from the schools of the Fourth Way.)

——*The Theory of Conscious Harmony*, Shambhala, Boulder/London, 1983

——*The Theory of Eternal Life*, Shambhala, Boulder/London, 1983

——*Spiegel des Lichts. Aus den Notizbüchern*, Plejaden, Boltersen, 1990. (A moving booklet full of wise sayings.)

Dukes, Paul, *The Unending Quest*, Cassell, London, 1950

Ebert, Andreas, and Rohr, Richard (editors), *Erfahrungen mit dem Enneagramm. Sich selbst und Gott begegnen*, Claudius, Munich, 1992. (This is a collection of essays by people involved in the Church, which attempts to make use of the Enneagramm for the purposes of organized religion. It also includes a personality test which can be ordered separately.)

Endres, Franz Carl, and Schimmel, Annemarie, *Das Mysterium der Zahl. Zahlensymbolik im Kulturvergleich*, Diederichs, Cologne, 1984

Franz, Marie-Louise von, *Puer Aeternus: a psychological study of the adult struggle*, Sigo Paperbacks, US, 1985

Fromm, Erich, *To Have or To Be*, Abacus, London, 1990

Goethe, Johann Wolfgang von, *Farbenlehre. Mit Einleitung und Kommentaren von Rudolf Steiner*, Verlag Freies Geistesleben, Stuttgart, 1979

Gurdjieff, G I, *The Struggle of the Magicians*, The Stourton Press, Capetown, 1957. (The only published edition of Gurdjieff's ballet.)

——*Views From The Real World*, Routledge & Kegan Paul, London, 1973 (out of print)

——*Beelzebub's Tales To His Grandson*, Routledge & Kegan Paul, London, 1950. (Gurdjieff's fundamental work, in which one can find all his ideas expressed. But it is very hard to understand without a commentary or help from a Gurdjieff group. A helpful commentary is the *Guide and Index to All and Everything (Anon)*, though it is unfortunately hard to get hold of.)

——*Meetings With Remarkable Men*, Routledge & Kegan Paul, London, 1963

——*Life Is Real Only Then, When 'I Am'*, Triangle Books, New York, 1975 (privately printed). This is a partly autobiographical work which was never completed.

——*Herald of Coming Good*, La Societé Anonyme des Editions de L'Quest, Angers

Hartmann, Thomas de, *Our Life with Mr. Gurdjieff*, Cooper Square Publications, New York, 1964. (Also in an extended and reworked edition, edited by Thomas C Daly and T A G Daly, Penguin Books, London, 1992. This later edition is much more informative than the original one of 1964 and the Harper Row edition of 1983.)

Hulme, Katheryn, *Undiscovered Country*, Little Brown & Co, Boston, 1966

Jaxon-Bear, Eli, *Die neun Zahlen des Lebens. Das Enneagram – Charakterfixierung und spirituelles Wachstum*, Knaur, Munich, 1989. (The author takes the Ichazo typology as her point of departure, and tries, in an often humorous way, to stimulate the reader to overcome his/her normal behaviour patterns.)

Jung, C G, *Collected Works*, Routledge, London, 1990

Jung, Emma, and von Franz, Marie-Louise, *Grail Legend*, Sigo Paperbacks, US, 1992

Kerenyi, Karl, *Die Mythologie der Griechen*, 2 vols, Deutscher Taschenbuch Verlag, Munich, 1976

Keyes, Margaret Frings, *The Enneagram Cats of Muir Beach*, Molysdatur, Muir Beach, 1990. (A very original, comical introduction to Ichazo's psychological typology.)

——*Transformiere deinen Schatten. Die Psychologie des Enneagrams*, Rowohlt, Reinbek, 1992. (A transaction-analytical view of Ichazo's typology.)

Keyserling, Arnold Graf, *Klaviatur des Denkens*, Vienna, self-published, 1971. (This and the following book can be regarded as an introduction – though very hard to understand – to the Neue Wiener Schule's (The New Vienna School) approach to Gurdjieff

——*Durch Sinnlichkeit zum Sinn. Die Sinne vermitteln die Wirklichkeit, die Sinnlichkeit führt zur Meisterung der fünf Sinne*, Bruno Martin, Südergesellen, 1986

Kheridan, David, *On a Spaceship With Beelzebub. By a Grandson of Gurdjieff*, Globe, New York, 1991

Kuchinsky, Saul, *Systematics. Search for Miraculous Management*, Claymont Communication, Charles Town/West Virginia, 1985. (A good introduction into the use of the Enneagram and related systems in business management. Includes an interesting interview with Bennett.)

Landau, Rom, *God Is My Adventure*, Ivor Nicholson & Watson, 1935

Leblanc, Georgette, *La Machine a Courage. Souvenirs*, Janin, Paris, 1947

Lefort, Rafael, *Die Lehrer Gurdjieffs. Reise zu den Sufimeistern*, Bruno Martin, Frankfurt, 1980 (out of print)

Leonard, Linda, *Töchter und Väter. Heilung und Chancen einer verletzten Beziehung*, Kösel, Munich, 1986

Levi, Eliphas, *Schlüssel zu den grossen Mysterien*, O W Barth, Weilheim, 1966

McCorkle, Beth, *The Gurdjieff Years 1929–1949: recollections* of *Louise March*, The Work Study Association, New York, 1990

Mansfield, Katherine, *Katherine Mansfield's Letters to John Middleton Murray 1913–1922*, Constable, London, 1951

Metz, Barbara, and Burchill, John, *The Enneagram and Prayer – Discovering Our True Self Before God*, Dimension Books, Denville/New York, 1987

Moore, James, 'The Enneagram: A Developmental Study' In: *Religion Today: A Journal of Contemporary Religions*, Vol. 5, No. 3

——*Gurdjieff and Mansfield*, Routledge & Kegan Paul, London, 1980

——*Gurdjieff. The Anatomy of a Myth. A Biography*, Element Books, Shaftesbury/Rockport, 1991. (A very good documentation of Gurdjieff's life, though in a somewhat mannered style. It contains previously unpublished documents; and photographs of, among other things, Gurdjieff's pupils.)

Mouravieff, Boris, 'Ouspensky, Gurdjieff et les fragments d'un enseignement inconnu'. In: *Revue Syntheses*, No. 138, Brussels, 1957. (An orthodox Christian interpretation of Gurdjieff's work)

——*Gnosis, Book One. Study and Commentaries on the Esoteric Tradition of Eastern Orthodoxy. Exotyeric Cycle*, Agora Press, Robertsbridge, 1989. (This doesn't contain anything much different from Ouspensky's *In Search Of the Miraculous*. Its approach, though, is rather insistently Christian.)

Müller, Lutz, *Der Held. Jeder ist dazu geboren*, Kreuz, Zürich, 1987

Natale, Frank, 'Die neun Persönlichkeitstypen. Das Modell der Göttinnen und Götter'. In: *Connection*, Niedertaufkirchen, 1992, 4/8/92 (in a series which was published between April and August 1992; it had little to do with Gurdjieff's ideas though)

Neue Wiener Schule (New Vienna School [Graf Keyserling]), *Im Jahr des Uranus. Wege des philosophioschen Handwerks.* (An unusual and poorly explained Enneagram system.)

Nicoll, Maurice, *The New Man*, Hermitage House, New York, 1951; Shambhala, Boulder, Colorado, 1981 (A study by

Jung's pupil Nicoll on the New Testament, from the view-point of the schools of the Fourth Way.)

Nicoll, Maurice, *Psychological Commentaries on the Teaching of Gurdjieff and Ouspensky*, Vols 1 and 2. Shambhala, Boulder, Colorado, 1952. (This and the following book provide the basis for a depth-psychology originating in Gurdjieff's teachings.)

——*Psychological Commentaries on the Teachings of Gurdjieff*, 6 vols, Vincent Stuart. London, 1950–1956

——*The Active Mind*, Hermitage House, New York, 1954

Norelli-Bachelet, Patrizia, *The Gnostic Circle: a synthesis*, Aeon Books, 1994. (A fundamental book on Enneagram astrology.)

Nott, C S, *Teachings of Gurdjieff: The Journal of a Pupil. An Account of Some Years with G I Gurdjieff and A R Orage in New York and at Fontainebleau-Avon*, Routledge & Kegan Paul, London, 1961. Also, Arkana, London, 1961 in paperback. (A good book, that is much concerned with Orage. From pages 125 to 216 it provides a good introduction to *Beelzebub's Tales*. It also gives many interesting details about the 'movements' and has photographs of these.)

——*Journey Through This World: The Second Journal of a Pupil. Including an Account of Meetings with G I Gurdjieff, A R Orage and P D Ouspensky*, Routledge & Kegan Paul, London

Oesterheld, Vivado, 'George Ivanowitsch Gurdjieff. Fragmente einer Geheimlehre'. In: *Connection*, Munich, Sept. 1988. (A very good, short overview. Unfortunately out of print.)

Olgivanna (O Lloyd Wright), 'The Last days of Katherine Mansfield'. In: *The Bookman*, New York, 1931, March 73/1, pages 6–13

Ouspensky, Peter Demian(ovich), *The Inner Circle*, St. Petersburg, 1913

——*Fragments of an Unknown Teaching*, Routledge & Kegan Paul, London, 1950

——*The Psychology of Man's Possible Evolution*, Hedgehog Press, London, 1950

——*The Fourth Way. A record of Talks and Answers to Questions*, Routledge & Kegan Paul, London, 1957. (A terribly dry standard work on the teachings of Gurdjieff and Ouspensky, but very thorough.)

——*In Search of the Miraculous*, Routledge & Kegan Paul, London, 1950. (Probably the best and most extensive description of Gurdjieff's teachings.)

Palmer, Helen, *Das Enneagram. Sich selbst und andere verstehen lernen*, Knaur, Munich, 1991. (Based on Ichazo's typology)

Paquet, Alphons, *Delphinische Wanderungen*, Drei Masken, Munich, 1922. (Paquet, a German Quaker, attempts in this book a short description of the 'movements'.)

Pauwells, Louis, *Gurdjieff der Magier*, Scherz, Bern/Munich, 1974. (A very subjective view of Gurdjieff.)

Peters, Fritz, *Boyhood with Gurdjieff*, Gollancz, London, 1964. (Easier to obtain through: Capra Press, Santa Barabara/Cal., 1980. Henry Miller compared this very gripping book to *Alice in Wonderland*. An old man recalls his early life with Gurdjieff in Fontainebleau. This book is full of stories and background information.)

——*Gurdjieff Remembered*, Samuel Weiser, New York, 1971

Phillips, Michael, *The Seven Laws of Money*, Random House, New York, 1974

Popoff, I B, *Gurdjieff: His Work on Myself . . . with Others . . . for the Work*, Vintage, New York, 1969

——*The Enneagramma of the Man of Unity*, New York, 1978

Rajneesh, Bhagwan (Osho), 'Bhagwan on Gurdjieff'. In: *Connection*, Munich, 1988, Sept. pages 9–13. (It is impossible to list here all of Rajneesh's references to Gurdjieff. They appear in many different lectures, question-and-answer sessions and in his books. Of particular note are: *Tao Three Treasures* (Vol. 2, p. 303), *Yaa-Hoo Mystic Rose* (Chapters 5, 8, 10, 29), *Mustard Seed* (p. 41), *Beyond Psychology* (Chapter 29) and *Transmission of the Lamp* (Nos. 14, 19, 20))

Random, Michel, *Les puissances du dedans: Luc Dietrich, Lanza del Vastyon, Rene Daumal, Gurdjieff*, Denoel, Paris, 1966

Reich, Wilhelm, *Character Analysis*, FS & G, 1980

Reyner, J H, *The Gurdjieff Inheritance*, Turnstone Press, Bath, 1985

Riso, Don Richard, *Personality Types: Using the Enneagram for Self-Discovery*, Houghton Mifflin, New York/London, 1995
——*Discovering Your Personality Type. The Enneagram Questionnaire*, Houghton Mifflin, New York/London, 1992
Rohr, Richard, and Ebert, Andreas, *Das Enneagram. Die neun Gesichter der Seele*, Claudius, Munich, 1989. (An attempt to lay claim to the Enneagram typology as a Christian methodology.)
——*Discovering the Enneagram. An ancient tool, a new spiritual journey*, Crossroad, New York, 1992
Sahihi, Arman, *Das neue Lexikon der Astrologie*, Ariston, Genf/Munich, 1991
Schneider, Sugata, 'Gurdjieff und seine Schüler. Schocks und Schmerzen eines werdended Bewusstseins'. In: *Connection*, Munich 1988, Sept. page 16 onwards
Schultz, Joachim, *Rhythmen der Sterne. Erscheinungen und Bewegungen von Sonne, Mond und Planeten*. Published by the Mathematisch-Astronomische Sektion am Goetheanum, Dornach: Philosophisch-Anthroposophischer Verlag, 1963
Seurat, Denis, 'A Visit to Gourdyev'. In: *Living Age*, London, 1934, Jan, 345/4408, pages 427–433
Sicuteri, Roberto, *Astrologie und Mythos. Mythen und Symbole im Spiegel der Tiefenpsychologie*, Aurum, Freiburg i. Br., 1983
Speeth, Kathleen Riordan, *The Gurdjieff Work*, And/Or Press, Berkeley, California, 1976
Staveley, A L, *Memoires of Gurdjieff*, Two Rivers Press, Aurora, Oregon, 1978
Steiger, Bruno, *Gurdjieff Argument*, Rowohlt, Reinbek, 1985
Steinbeck, John, *Acts of King Arthur and His Noble Knights*, Mandarin Press, London, 1992
Tilley, Basil, *Letters from Paris and England 1947–1949*, self-published (Phene Press), 1981
Travers, P L, *George Ivanovitch Gurdjieff*, Traditional Studies Press, Toronto, 1973
Vayesse, Jean, *Towards Awakening*, Arkana, London/New York, 1988
Vollmar, Klausbernd, *Journey Through the Chakras*, Gateway Books, Bath, 1987

——'Neue Bücher zum Enneagramm'. In: *Hologramm*, Südergesellen, 1989, 16/58

——'Neun Persönlichkeitstypen'. In: *Esotera*, Freiburg, 1990, 6/90

——*Chakren – Lebenskraft und Lebensfreude aus der eigenen Mitte*, Gräfe und Unzer, Munich, 1991

——*Farben – Ihre natürliche Heilkraft*, Gräfe und Unzer, Munich, 1992

——'Die Intelligenz des Körpers. Ganzheitliches Lernen nach Gurdjieff'. In: *Connection Special*, Niedertaufkirchen, 1992, 1/92, pages 76–79

——*Das Geheimnis der Farbe Rot. Einladung zum Spiel mit dem Feuer. Ein Lese- und Übungsbuch zur Symbolik und Psychologie einer starken Farbe*, Edition Tramontane, Bad Münstereifel, 1992

——'Der mit dem Ego spielt'. In: *Connection*, Niedertaufkirchen, 1993, 1/93, pages 28–30

Wagner, Jerome P, *A descriptive, reliability and validity study of the Enneagram personality typology*. Loyola University, Chicago, 1981

Walberg, Michael, *Gurdjieff. An Approach to his Ideas*, Routledge & Kegan Paul, London, 1981

Walker, Kenneth, *A Study of Gurdjieff's Teaching*, Jonathan Cape, London, 1957

Webb, James, *The Harmonious Circle: The Lives and Work of G I Gurdjieff, P D Ouspensky, and Their Followers*, Thames and Hudson, London, 1980

Welch, Louise, *Orage with Gurdjieff in America*, Routledge & Kegan Paul, London/Boston, 1982

Wilson, Colin, *The War Against Sleep. The Philosophy of Gurdjieff*, The Aquarian Press, Northamptonshire, 1980. (Very good bibliography)

Wolff, Edwin, *Episodes with Gurdjieff*, Far West Press, San Francisco, 1974

Young, James Carruthers, 'An Experiment at Fontainebleau: A Personal Reminiscence'. In: *New Adelphi 1927*, Sept. I/1, pages 26–40

Zuber, René, *Wer Sind Sie Herr Gurdjieff?* Sphinx, Basel, 1981. (A short description of Gurdjieff's life and teachings.)

The author is available to give courses, workshops and lectures on the Enneagram. For details please contact:

Klausbernd Vollmar (Dipl. Psych.)
Cobblestones
Cley next the Sea
Norfolk DR25 7RE
Great Britain
Fax + Tel: 01263 740 304